INTERNATIONAL CONFERENCE ON
ALL-WHEEL DRIVE

IMechE CONFERENCE PUBLICATIONS 1986-1

Sponsored by
The Automobile Division of
The Institution of Mechanical Engineers

Co-sponsored by
Verein Deutscher Ingenieure

5-6 March 1986
The Institution of Mechanical Engineers
Birdcage Walk
London

Published for
The Institution of Mechanical Engineers
by Mechanical Engineering Publications Limited
LONDON

Proceedings of the Institution of Mechanical Engineers

First published 1986

This publication is copyright under the Berne Convention and the International Copyright Convention. Apart from any fair dealing for the purpose of private study, research, criticism or review, as permitted under the Copyright Act 1956, no part may be reproduced, stored in a retrieval system, or transmitted in any form or by any means, electronic, electrical, chemical, mechanical, photocopying, recording or otherwise, without the prior permission of the copyright owners. Inquiries should be addressed to: The Senior Co-ordinating Editor, Mechanical Engineering Publications Limited, PO Box 24, Northgate Avenue, Bury St Edmunds, Suffolk IP32 6BW

© The Institution of Mechanical Engineers 1986

ISBN 0 85298 588 6

The Publishers are not responsible for any statement made in this publication. Data, discussion and conclusions developed by authors are for information only and are not intended for use without independent substantiating investigation on the part of potential users.

Printed by Waveney Print Services Ltd, Beccles, Suffolk

CONTENTS

The Institution of Mechanical Engineers

The primary purpose of the 76,000-member Institution of Mechanical Engineers, formed in 1847, has always been and remains the promotion of standards of excellence in British mechanical engineering and a high level of professional development, competence and conduct among aspiring and practising members. Membership of IMechE is highly regarded by employers, both within the UK and overseas, who recognise that its carefully monitored academic training and responsibility standards are second to none. Indeed they offer incontrovertible evidence of a sound formation and continuing development in career progression.

In pursuit of its aim of attracting suitably qualified youngsters into the profession — in adequate numbers to meet the country's future needs — and of assisting established Chartered Mechanical Engineers to update their knowledge of technological developments — in areas such as CADCAM, robotics and FMS, for example — the IMechE offers a comprehensive range of services and activities. Among these, to name but a few, are symposia, courses, conferences, lectures, competitions, surveys, publications, awards and prizes. A Library containing 150,000 books and periodicals and an Information Service which uses a computer terminal linked to databases in Europe and the USA are among the facilities provided by the Institution.

If you wish to know more about the membership requirements or about the Institution's activities listed above — or have a friend or relative who might be interested — telephone or write to IMechE in the first instance and ask for a copy of our colour 'at a glance' leaflet. This provides fuller details and the contact points — both at the London HQ and IMechE's Bury St Edmunds office — for various aspects of the organisation's operation. Specifically it contains a tear-off slip through which more information on any of the membership grades (Student, Graduate, Associate Member, Member and Fellow) may be obtained.

Corporate members of the Institution are able to use the coveted letters 'CEng, MIMechE' or 'CEng, FIMechE' after their name, designations instantly recognised by, and highly acceptable to, employers in the field of engineering. There is no way other than by membership through which they can be obtained!

Introductory paper

F SHAW, CEng, FIMechE

SYNOPSIS   The purpose of this paper is to set the scene and provide a discussion catalyst through a short history of problems and their solutions encountered in all-wheel drive engineering, together with an attempt to forecast future trends.

1   THE PAST

Figure 1 shows the most effective all-wheel drive vehicle, with all-wheel steering and all-wheel brakes. Could this specification, achieved differently, be the best suited to future requirements?

All-wheel drive has been confined almost entirely to trucks and special purpose vehicles. In particular, cross-country and off-road types, having an on-road facility, but where the prime purpose has been essentially 'work-horse'. In recent years these have been joined by high performance glamour vehicles where the main use is on the road, with a cross-country facility. When on-road use is predominant it is normal to incorporate permanent four-wheel drive, whereas in genuine work-horse vehicles it is customary to bring in the front axle drive when leaving the road.

During this conference the reason may become clear, and will perhaps underline the belief that a policy of designing a four-wheel drive system for luxury cars and then, for purely economic purposes, applying the same system to genuine work-horse vehicles is inevitably going to reduce the fitness for purpose of the latter. Conditions applying to utility vehicles differ from those of a luxury car to such an extent that they are not compatible.

In considering the parameters for designing four-wheel drive vehicles it would be wrong to depart too far from the principles developed, and well proven, over a century of motor car engineering. On the other hand, the circumstances under which the parameters were fixed are different in many ways.

It is still true that the absolute limit for acceleration, braking and cornering capabilities for any vehicle is set by the adhesion between the tyre and the surface on which it runs. The possible surface condition for off-road vehicles bears no resemblance for that normally met in a motor car. In front or rear wheel drive motor cars the location of the engine, and the weight distribution, is of extreme importance. With the logically correct drive on all wheels this becomes relatively unimportant.

The ideal is to incorporate an intermediate differential between the axles, in addition to those in the axles. This permits drive at all wheels at the same time, and allows for the front and rear axles rotating at different speeds. Figure 2 indicates why wind-up is not so important in cross-country vehicles, and also the sort of shock loads which can be expected when an airborne vehicle hits the ground.

Systems such as that used in the Jensen F.F. motor car (developed by Harry Ferguson Research Ltd) control the bias in the intermediate differential. Sometimes a free-wheel device is introduced in the front drive to prevent wind-up in the transmission shafts and it is necessary to lock up the free-wheel when using the vehicle in reverse. There is an ingenious selector mechanism to accomplish this. In locking up a free-wheel it is important that a high torque is not applied at the moment of lock-up otherwise it cannot be unlocked until the same magnitude and direction of torque is reapplied. This of course applies only to a dog type lock-up.

Viscous couplings and limited slip differentials are used to ensure drive at all wheels. Mechanical types of spin resistant differentials provide some drive at each wheel.

There was a case recently of a vehicle, so fitted, which ran rings round its competitors in muddy conditions and these units should be given serious consideration. Experience showed, however, that though these differentials gave excellent results in low adhesion conditions they can be intolerable on a good road surface unless the vehicle is running in a dead straight line ahead.

With four-wheel drive, if the front wheels drop into a ditch, they climb out instead of being forced deeper into it by the drive from the rear wheels. This benefit can play against an unwary driver when moving along a forest path with the wheels in deep soft ruts. In a four-wheel drive vehicle it is virtually impossible to be sure of the angular position of the front wheels because even if they are on full lock the rear wheels will push them through the rut. When a section of rut with weak walls is reached the front drive takes over and the vehicle moves sideways into the trees at an alarming rate. The spinning steering wheel will probably remove your thumb at the same time. The pushing advantage can be taken still further by providing a powered drive to a trailer having a live axle driven at the same speed as the vehicle axles as shown in Figure 3. It is fascinating to see the vehicle pulling the trailer, and suddenly the vehicle loses traction on a sand dune, and the trailer pushes the vehicle out of trouble.

Work-horse vehicles must have as many power take-off points as possible. At the rear, to drive towed equipment (Figure 4) and for mobile workshops (Figure 5). At the side and below, for pumps and generators etc. At the front, for winches and fire pumps. Winches are not only for hauling loads and erecting telephone posts, but can be used for vehicle recovery and, equally important with the aid of a rope and a tree, for recovering one's own vehicle.

Considering the strength of parts in the transmission, and in the vehicle springs and associated suspension components, it must always be borne in mind that the torque available from the engine, through the low ratios, cannot always be utilized and a thorough understanding of the torque being applied is essential to avoid over engineering, and to make certain that there are no high shock loads of which one may be unaware. It is absolutely essential that a vehicle is instrumented and the torque in all loaded parts quantified under controlled fully operational conditions. These acquired figures must be recorded, plotted and analysed.

It has been practice to calculate anticipated service life using empirical formulae and this was accurate enough for cars where the conditions under which they operate are reliably predictable. Considering the infinite variation, and the virtual ill-use, of work-horse vehicles, it becomes clear that no single empirical values can satisfy all cases and realistic, measured values must be acquired.

Figures 6 to 11 illustrate some of the multiple uses to which work-horse vehicles are subjected, in order to emphasise the special nature of this type of vehicle.

Figure 6 shows a vehicle towing a 105 m.m. field gun which bounces and yaws, putting extraordinary loads on the vehicle rear wheels. With locked up four-wheel drive it is possible to put the whole torque on one axle, even if only momentarily.

Figure 7 is a conversion requiring no comment except that it is one of many such conversions.

Figure 8 gives an indication of the sort of power take-off required, whilst Figure 9 demonstrates the kind of use to which the vehicle may be adapted in under-developed countries. The vehicle itself must travel through desert, or rough jungle terrain, and then be set up to give entertainment, or instructional film shows, generating its own power. Military use requires very rough terrain facility, and absolute dependability.

Figures 10 and 11 show conversions which emphasise the impossibility of using luxury car systems in 'do anything go anywhere' vehicles.

Figure 12 illustrates a floatation conversion for jungle areas. Originally this vehicle was fitted with a propeller driven by the rear power take-off, but it was shown that the rotating wheels impelled the 'craft' fast enough for the purpose.

Figure 13 shows how vehicles are made to run on rails with rimmed wheels overhanging the hub bearings by up to 14 inches each side, according to the gauge of the particular country. This puts in perspective the problems one may

encounter in engineering these vehicles. No failures were experienced and the customer preferred to purchase a lot of 4x4 vehicles than one shunting engine.

Chains can be used successfully in transfer boxes, and there is little to choose between roller chains and inverted tooth chains, although it is just possible that the inverted tooth chain might better suit the higher speeds of luxury utility vehicles and motor cars.

Figure 14 shows a prototype tractor based on an existing 4x4 chassis having driving axles front and rear, with inter-linked four wheel steering, to minimise ploughing waste when turning at the end of furrows. The wheel centres were normally seven inches below the axle centre line with a reduction gear. The casing could be inverted so that the wheel centres would be above the axle centre line. This could be done on all four wheels, or on one side only for working on the side of a hill.

The Spiker car had four-wheel drive and four-wheel brakes in 1903. The idea was as right then as it is now, so what went wrong? One can only assume that this is one prime example of not doing it right initially and killing the idea for years.

2 THE CURRENT SITUATION AND THE IMMEDIATE FUTURE

The requirement for 4x4 vehicles for 'on' and 'off' road use, with cross-country performance, and suitable for work-horse duties, will continue, and operators will expect them to be improved, but without over sophistication.

Four-wheel drive and four-wheel steering are inevitable requirements for high quality motor cars (and eventually all cars) in the late 1990s, and the highest possible degree of sophistication will be demanded.

Can the requirements of cars and work-horse vehicles ever be met by a compromise solution? This would appear to be most unlikely.

Figure 15 shows a typical four-wheel drive arrangement in use for off-road and cross-country vehicles from the late 1930s. There has been little departure from this, and for many years the Willys Jeep, and later the Land-Rover, dominated the world market using basically the same layout.

Although designers have been concerned about the multiplicity of knobs and levers associated with these basic vehicles, it must be remembered that most operators are accustomed to agricultural machinery with similar complications and it matters little to them. Neither are they too particular about car type quietness or speed, but they are very concerned about dependability and total fitness for purpose.

Unnecessary specification changes should be avoided because operators expect the vehicles to remain in use for many years, and that spares will be readily available. A considerable amount of cannibalisation from vehicle to vehicle is also practised.

Many owners produce specialised auxiliary equipment for the vehicle and anticipate these to be capable of continued use, even in replacement vehicles.

Basic vehicles of this type have fundamental failings which have been tolerated, though reluctantly, by customers. Many attempts have been made to eradicate them but some remain to this day.

It has often been said that a four by four vehicle is a mass of transmission equipment, held together by girders, and powered by an engine. Figure 16 shows the heart of this system in the gearbox and transfer gear.

The change down, from high to low ratio in the transfer box, has never been easy in a moving vehicle. There have been many attempts to introduce a normal baulking type synchromesh unit, but the inertia of the parts and the magnitude of the ratio step has always made this impractical. Even multi-cone systems, such as those developed by Porsche and Smiths Industries, amongst others, could not cope. Various dog arrangements have been tried without real success. One of the most promising was the Sinclair self shifting mechanism (developed by Fluidrive Engineering) because of its ability to change ratios without letting go of the drive. The very feature of not passing through neutral was against it because of the need for a neutral position in the transfer system. Also the S.S.S. unit depends on torque reversal, giving 'off power' changes up, and power changes down, which hardly suits cross-country conditions.

Of late there has been much progress made in simple transfer selection, though only a non-dogging type of coupling could ever be completely successful. Most of the effective ones are, in fact, hydraulic or friction types.

Another failing of the cog box system is the danger associated with jumping out of engagement. When descending a steep, slippery slope, and depending on engine retardation through the low range gears, there is the possibility of the drive becoming disengaged, allowing the vehicle to run away at an increasing speed. Re-engagement of the drive in motion is very difficult and applying the wheel brakes merely converts the vehicle into an out of control sledge.

Angled teeth and stepped splines have been introduced to prevent gear disengagement and, though these were tolerably successful, they were never completely reliable. With positive evidence of disengagement under load, be it drive or over-run, the problem is not difficult to solve, but often there is a tendency to move out of engagement in the 'no load' condition and this nullifies the anti-jump out device.

Extended use of reverse gear when climbing out of sloping mine shafts, or crop spraying in confined rows, can cause a problem with the reverse idler wheel for both lubrication and jump out. Police vehicles are often called upon to reverse four or five miles at speed on the hard shoulder of motorways.

The best cure for reverse jump-out is the use of a needle bearing pack in the idler gear having a few minutes 'tweak' in the cages. After reversing the vehicle, and returning to neutral, the reverse gear must be fully disengaged otherwise the feature which prevents jump-out may pull the idler back into engagement leaving the selector mechanism in neutral.

In addition to adverse lubrication conditions when reversing for considerable distances the vehicle could be operating in situations, and at angles, where the normal 'dip and splash' lubrication is ineffective. In surveying it may be necessary to take theodolite readings with the vehicle stationary on a compound slope of perhaps 45x45 degrees with the primary and lay-shafts rotating in a part of the box devoid of oil. These problems are compensated for by the addition of catchers, stirrers and channels to direct the oil to where it is required, or by the addition of a simple oil pump. This solution is favoured because, in addition to curing boundary lubrication problems, it gives extended tooth life and permits higher loadings.

It has been usual to relate the gear box ratios to the axle strength by mandatory selection of four-wheel drive when in low range, thus permitting the use of a smaller axle at the rear. Very often the same size as the front axle which, in the case of a Scott banjo construction, allows a switch of running gear should the rear axle fail.

Provided they are selected properly, axles give few problems. The only troubles are usually associated with lubrication because of two fundamental differences when compared with motor cars. The front axle crown wheel rotates in a direction opposite to normal. Whilst this poses no problem gear-wise, care must be taken to ensure proper lubrication for the pinion bearings. In all cases it has been possible to modify the oil gallery and scrapers to ensure satisfactory flow, but it is essential to check this flow through a window cut in the case, at low and high speeds of rotation, and at all intermediate speeds, both ascending and descending.

The other feature requiring attention is the thrust faces of the differential gears because the loads are usually higher than in cars, and certainly the operating conditions are such that the differential works more frequently due to the terrain and the greater incidence of wheel lift.

Tyre wear was expected to be a problem, particularly on the front pair, and a free wheeling device and expensive constant velocity joints were thought to be necessary. Though vehicles were originally produced with these features, and the mathematics of four-wheel drive theory would totally support it, a sloppy dog in the front drive engagement, and ordinary universal joints at the front road wheels proved to be satisfactory for utility and work-horse vehicles.

In developing the Range-Rover, the front drive arrangement with the sloppy dog was still reasonably acceptable but constant velocity joints at the front wheels were essential for the higher speeds and increased performance and quality. More attention was required to improve out of balance forces inherent in the drive line.

Eventually a great improvement was achieved by introducing the intermediate differential and permanent four-wheel drive. The sloppy dog was used for locking up the differential in adverse conditions, though it was rarely necessary.

Simple unlocked differentials in both axles, and an intermediate differential, copes well enough with most conditions, except where there is total loss of traction, as on wet ice. A thorough investigation is required into the real value of locking or limited slip differentials in cross-country vehicles. Certainly they have proved very successful in high-powered car rear axles. Indications are that they may have an even more important part to play in motor cars with four-wheel drive.

There are clear signs that future designers need to follow two courses. One for four-wheel drive cars, where elegance of performance, reduced weight, and silence of operation will be paramount; and the other for work-horse vehicles where low range ratios are required, with longer life dependability, and ruggedness, coupled with adaptability and simple 'in the field' servicing.

In attempting a common solution for cars and utility vehicles there are requirements for each which makes a compromise unacceptable. The author recalls, with considerable regret, being persuaded, against his better judgement, to compromise a new gear box and transfer gear for the Range-Rover because money was not available for both a light unit designed specifically for the more elegant vehicle, and also for a more rugged unit required for a large forward control military vehicle (Figures 10 and 11).

No one ever broke the box in a Range-Rover, but it lacked the elegance which the vehicle deserved in its own right. Later a custom made gearbox was introduced and Range-Rover was much improved.

Ground clearance needs are entirely different between cars and off-road vehicles, and although operators will not accept poor quality gear selection in commercial vehicles, it would be expected that for luxury cars, an even higher standard would be demanded.

It is conceivable that the introduction of systems such as automatic transmissions utilizing a viscous coupling in the transfer section, or even hydraulic drive with oil vane motors at each wheel, could eliminate a lot of problems, and at the same time go a long way towards achieving a satisfactory compromise between work-horse vehicles and luxury motor cars.

Transmission designers should be vigilant about undue pressures from financial controllers towards any compromise which may be regretted later, because it could result in condemning the use of four-wheel drive, and four-wheel steering, in good quality motor cars for years to come, simply because it isn't done right on initial introduction. In the interest of safety alone this must not happen. Nor must the ruggedness, and fitness for purpose, of the off-road vehicle be sacrificed on the altar of expediency.

Fitness for purpose is of paramount importance in these two differing vehicles and decisions must be made based on engineering principles. The only real thing they have in common is that they both drive all wheels. The only thing common between whisky and water is that they are both liquid.

3 THE OUTLOOK FOR MOTOR CARS

Whilst it is true that everything on post-war cars already existed, in some form, on some car, in the twenty years prior to 1939 it is equally true that the rate of development since the 1960s has been phenomenal. Most of all due to customer acceptance that features once considered to be expensive options should be standard fitment.

Buyers are now entering an era of the automobile which will make the previous post-war progress seem insignificant. After twenty years of introducing unimaginative, mundane, features (largely gimmicky) manufacturers are now attracting customers with mouth watering, high technological innovations.

Moving into the 1990s cars and commercial vehicles will evolve at an astonishing rate. Manufacturers in every industrialised nation have been investing in well directed R&D, and in factories capable of taking full advantage of the new technologies, and getting them into production and into vehicles with the least delay.

Cars will become even more expensive as customers expect, and insist upon, the latest technological improvements. The more expensive cars will be virtually indistinguishable from each other as the optimum design is adopted for aerodynamic perfection, but each car will be highly individual otherwise, with manufacturers competing in providing technological improvements.

The greater use of computer controls will cause the car to respond better to the driver's instructions, and adjust to road conditions. Cars will be more exciting to drive, more economical in performance, and less trouble to own and maintain.

With the projected improvements in the cost, comfort, and convenience of public transport it will be necessary for manufacturers of motor cars to woo the motorist and do everything possible to restore the fun and adventure of motoring.

Micro-processor controls are transforming brakes, steering, suspensions, engines, and transmissions. Anti-lock brakes are the finest contribution to safety and their relationship to all-wheel drive should not be overlooked. The main advantage is that the driver can safely change direction whilst braking sharply, thus avoiding obstacles and other skidding cars, during a panic stop.

An equally important advance in safety and handling will be in forms of four-wheel drive, and four-wheel steering. Basic designs of four-wheel drive are already available on fun vehicles and a few cars. They are available, of course, on off-road vehicles. Ford, Audi, and others are already offering sophisticated systems. B.M.W., Porsche, and Austin Rover will soon introduce their own versions.

The idea of combining four-wheel drive and anti-lock brakes to attain the best possible adhesion at each wheel, under all conditions, is well advanced. Coupled with four-wheel steering, this could be very exciting.

Mazda cars introduced four-wheel steering on a prototype, and other companies have investigated the possibilities. Four-wheel steering enables the designer to extend the wheelbase, whilst allowing the car to turn on an old-fashioned sixpence at slow speeds, and handle more smoothly at high speeds. Mazda's system used a computer to adjust the magnitude and direction of steering applied to the rear wheels according to the car's speed. When the car is moving slowly, they swivel in a direction opposite to the front wheels, permitting the car to make tight turns. As the speed increases the rear wheels' swivel is reduced progressively, and at about 25 m.p.h. barely exists. At higher speeds they begin to swivel slightly in the same direction as the front wheels. The car moves sideways smoothly, and easily.

Four-wheel steering could initially have an acceptable on-cost and is a natural partner to four-wheel drive and the anti-lock brake system.

There is no doubt that the improvements made in the efficiency, cleanliness, and size of the petrol engine over the past years has ensured that it is here to stay as the prime mover, and the next few years should see even more improvements in performance. The transmission designer must, therefore, continue to design and develop drive-line systems for the improved petrol engines in motor cars, coupled with gearboxes having the maximum of automaticity in operation. Whether they be old-fashioned manual layshaft boxes with electronic brains, or sophisticated new designs, they will make certain that the engine/vehicle relationship is at peak efficiency at all times, and the drive-line must be engineered to take full advantage of this available power.

Four-wheel drive, four-wheel steering, and anti-lock brakes, probably coupled with a regenerative system, would appear to be the package most likely to achieve the objective of putting the most torque on the ground to the best advantage.

REFERENCES

I.Mech.E.
Drive line 70. proc. 1969-70 vol.184
Drive line 84. proc. 1984-]
Acknowledgements to Land-Rover Ltd for permission to reproduce illustrations.

Fig 2   Shock loads

Fig 3   Powered trailer

Fig 1   All wheel drive/steer and brakes

Fig 4   Crop spraying

Fig 5   Mobile workshop

Fig 8   Power take-off use

Fig 6   Towing a field gun

Fig 9   A mobile cinema

Fig 7   A tough conversion

Fig 10   Forward control conversion

Fig 11 Tracked vehicle

Fig 14 Four-wheel drive/four-wheel steered tractor

Fig 12 A flotation conversion

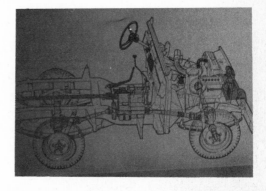

Fig 15 Typical four-wheel drive layout

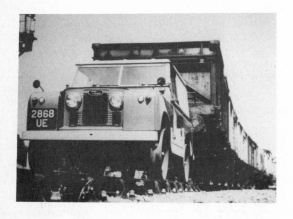

Fig 13 As a shunting engine

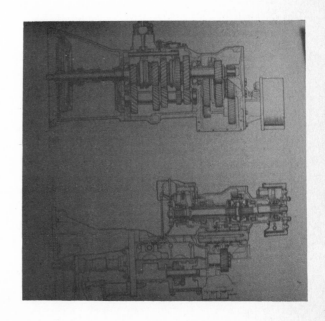

Fig 16 Typical gearbox and transfer gear

An assessment of future markets for cars with four-wheel drive systems

G S KVARNSTRÖM and L F SOMLOI, CEng
GKN/Uni-Cardan Aktiengesellschaft, Sieburg, West Germany

INTRODUCTION

The market for enhanced traction systems, i.e. limited slip differentials and 4WD-systems is expected to expand rapidly as a result of new market and competitive forces in USA/Canada, Japan and Western Europe. A detailed assessment of future 4WD development in Japan and USA/Canada will not, however, be given.

It is evident that the expected Enhanced Traction Systems (ETS) trends differ according to geographical areas and vehicle classes. Whereas the following analysis and forecasts have been made with reference to car classes some comments as to the car classification system applied should be made. We have adopted the following classification system. (See Table 1) The micro-class A includes cars such as Fiat Panda and Citroen 2CV, the mini-class B cars like Ford Fiesta, Fiat Uno and the lower medium class C Ford Escort, Opel Kadett and Maestro. The medium class C/D includes cars such as Ford Sierra, Opel Ascona and Renault 18, the upper medium class D covers such cars as Audi 100, BMW 3 and Ford Granada/Scorpio, the large and executive class E covers BMW 5, the Mercedes W124 and Opel Senator and finally the sports class G includes cars such as Audi Quattro and BMW 6.

Our assessment of the future 4WD markets has taken into consideration 4WD car trends, past trends of major options such as automatic transmission and anti-skid systems, and also information available to us as a main driveline component supplier, as well as information received through industry interviews.

APPLICATION SEGMENTS - 4WD TRENDS
(FIG 1)

The enhanced traction systems market is made up of several application segments of which 4 segments refer to 4WD and 1 segment to improved 2WD. The original application segment 'heavy duty - dedicated off road -' include all terrain vehicles such as AMC Jeep, Landrover and Landcruiser. A spin-off development of the heavy duty dedicated off road Jeep-type vehicles are the 'light duty - mixed use off-road' Jeep-type vehicles represented for example by Range Rover, Chevy Blazer and Jimmy, Ford Bronco, Cherokee 4x4 and Mercedes Benz G-series.

A further development is clearly recognizable in the application segment 'all conditions', which includes compact/micros, small to luxury passenger cars as well as pick-ups and vans. 4WD offerings in the market include in the class A compact/micro Fiat Panda and in class C Toyota Tercel, Alfa 33 and Subaru Sedan and Super Station, in class C/D Renault 18, VW Variant, Audi 80 and 90 and Ford Sierra. Audi 100 and and Audi 100 Avant are found in the D-class, as well as Audi Coupe and AMC Eagle. Finally, in the E-class Audi 200 and DB 300 TE are so far available as 4WD.

Another spin-off development is found in the performance cars with Audi Quattro, later followed by Porsche 959 and Ferrari, as well as Lancia Delta - all in class G - but performance cars with 4WD are also available in class B represented by Citroen Visa and Peugeot 205.

Attention shoud be given to the limited slip differential where improved traction of 2WD cars is concerned. Originally LSD's were applied on exclusive sports cars such as Aston Martin, Daimler, Lamborghini, Porsche 911, de Tomaso and many other. Recent developments indicate a growing market for limited slip and differentials for standard passenger cars in classes C-E. Not only the conventional plate type limited slip differential is available in the market, but in addition, new technologies are emerging such as Gleason Torsen worm gear type LSD and GKN Viscodrive LSD.

ENHANCED TRACTION SYSTEMS - AN ATTEMPT TO CATEGORIZE SYSTEMS FOR IMPROVED TRACTION OF 'ALL CONDITIONS' PASSENGER CARS

(FIG 2)

Following the classification of vehicles from large heavy duty vehicles to small family cars, we have made an attempt to classify 4WD systems for 'all conditions' passenger cars.

With enhanced traction systems we refer to systems, which are superior to the traditional rear wheel drive and front wheel drive, and range from various LSD-solutions for 2WD cars to a multiple range of 4WD systems.

The Japanese car producers have so far introduced cars with part-time systems in Western Europe. Some West European producers have concentrated on the relatively low priced part-time systems. With part-time systems we are referring to systems which are only being engaged part of the driving time and then, of course, only when required.

The multiple range of emerging 4WD part-time systems, make it necessary to distinguish between manually engageable systems and systems which are automatically engaged. Emerging automatic part-time systems include Visco-type coupling systems -such as being launched by Volkswagen - and sophisticated computer-controlled variable slip multi-disc couplings, as well as a new automatically operated mechanical coupling, which also could be attractive for the downscale car market from a price compatibility point of view.

We have therefore chosen to classify the manually engageable systems as 'On Demand Part-time systems' or 'ODPT' and the automatically engageable part-time systems as 'Automatic Part-time systems' or abbreviated 'AUPT'.

We have classified the permanently engaged systems as 'Constant 4WD or abbreviated 'CO'.

FORECAST GROWTH OF ANNUAL WORLD 4WD PRODUCTION 1984-1994 BY VEHICLE SEGMENTS

(FIG 3)

Present demand is mainly concentrated in 3 vehicle segments,

- heavy duty-utilites/Jeeps

- light duty-utilites/Jeeps

- all conditions incl. passenger cars, compact/micros and small vans.

The increasing demand for improved traction is reflected in higher sales of 4WD as well as LSD, particularly in Japan and the USA. This trend is also noticeable in Europe, though not so much in off-road and competition vehicles but, primarily, in all conditions driving passenger cars. The background to the demand in Western Europe is to be found in an increased awareness of the importance of safety and comfort, which also has been stimulated by deteriorating winter road conditions with less salt on roads and less public service, as well as by increased leisure with more time for outdoor activities such as skiing, trailer-boating camping and 'caravaning'.

We expect a rapid development in 4WD production from the 1984 figure of 2.2 million units, of which heavy utilities/Jeeps are estimated to be 0.2 million, light utilities 0.8 million, all conditions 1.2 million to a 1989 volume of 2.8 million units allocated to heavy utilities/jeeps 0.2 million, light utilities 0.8 million, all conditions 1.8 million, and anticipate a 1994 figure of 3.8 million units distributed between heavy utilities/jeeps 0.3 million, light utilities 0.8 million, all conditions 2.7 million.

The 'all conditions' are, thus, increasing from somewhat more than one million 1984 to close to 3 million by 1994. We expect the 4WD market to gain momentum during the next few years and to then rapidly increase in the late 80's and beginning of the 90's. In our opinion, rapid growth will take place in all major market areas - Japan, USA/Canada and Western Europe.

In Western Europe we expect that the production of all conditions cars with 4WD as standard or option by 1994 will be 5% of total production or close to 0.6 million cars. We consider this estimate to be extremely cautious and it is not unlikely that the production of 4WD all conditions cars could reach 7-8% of total production.

The very high 4WD penetration in USA/Canada, approximately 1 million vehicles, is almost exclusively centered around the heavy to light duty jeep-type vehicles. The development of all conditions 4WD passenger cars in USA has, however, started and we expect that the 4WD market will gain momentum in this area and in 1994 amount to 3% 4WD production or close to 0.3 million passenger cars. Expected market development through 4WD imports as well as stimulation through emerging 4WD technologies may, however, push domestic production closer to 5%.

The 4WD demand in the Japanese market has increased rapidly over the last few years and we expect 10% of the passenger car production in 1984 to be 4WD cars or approx. 0.8 million cars. Some analysts in Japan indicate the 10% 4WD-share of the total production to be realistic already at the end of the 80's.

A 4WD production in 1994 of 5% in Western Europe, 3% in the USA/Canada and 10% in Japan would mean an average of 6% for the Western world production of passenger cars. The high powered cars i.e. cars with a low weight to power ratio should, in our opinion, be a prime prospect for enhanced traction through LSD or 4WD, 23% of the cars produced in Western Europe have a weight to power ratio of less than 15 kg/kW. The high powered cars are currently available in class B with 7% and increasing throughout the classes to a high 79% figure in class G in Western Europe. In USA/Canada the high powered cars are found in the sub compacts with a 30% share and decreasing to 6% in the luxury class. The weight of the full-size American cars allows big engines without any significant loss of traction. The smaller European cars are more sensitive to powerful engines and would then require traction improvement.

PRICE COMPATIBILITY OF OPTIONS

(FIG 4)

When analyzing the market opportunities for 4WD, we have to consider and deal with the price sensitivity of the 4WD systems offered.

This could be effected in two different ways

- the option pricing curve over years of market acceptance.

- the option price relative to base vehicle price.

We have, on our analysis, chosen to relate the option prices to the base vehicle prices in 1985 prices in West Germany.

The incremental prices in percentage of car prices for 4WD options relative to other major options are shown in Fig 4.

Hydraulic power steering is offered for cars in the C-class upwards and starting at 8% in that class and decreasing to approx. 2% in the G-class. Automatic transmission is only available from the C-class upwards and starting at 11% in that class and decreasing to 3-4% in the G-class. Air conditioning is offered at 14% in the C-class and 6% in the G-class. Anti-skid systems are offered in the C/D-class and upwards, at 14% in the C/D-class and decreasing to 7% in the G-class. Limited slip differentials for enhanced traction are offered from the C-class and upwards, starting at 5% in the C-class and decreasing to 1% in the G-class. Those incremental price percentages for LSD refer to the conventional plate type limited slip differential or Viscodrive.

Of the 4WD options offered by European car manufacturers the ODPT systems are, for example, offered in Fiat Panda in class A with an incremental price percentage of 30% plus, to Alfa Romeo 33 in class C at 18%, both cars then being offered with a rigid beam rear axle. The constant 4WD-systems are offered from class C/D with Audi 80 and Ford Sierra with an incremental percentage of more than 30%, and ranging to the Audi 200 series in the E-class with an option price of approx. 17%. The high incremental price percentages for the 4WD options currently offered, would most likely prevent a rapid development of the 4WD market. New optimized enhanced traction systems with lower costs to the OEMs and lower installation costs with this option provided for in the base vehicle design, are a prerequisite for a deeper 4WD market penetration in Western Europe. That includes production compatibility of systems to allow the 4WD componentry to be assembled if possible on the same production line as 2WD cars. Such systems are expected to emerge in the market and are expected to be offered to the OEM's at a cost which allows a lower incremental price percentage than currently offered systems. That would allow the OEM's to offer these new 4WD options at a lower price in the market, and make 4WD-systems from 'On Demand Part-time', 'Automatic Part-time' and 'Constant' 4WD-systems competitive with other major options such as air conditioning and automatic transmission, thus allowing a broader buyer acceptance of the 4WD option.

4WD ENTRIES IN THE MARKET

(FIG 5)

The 4WD proliferation in Western Europe is already quite impressive with 24 4WD models in the market. 4WD models are available in all classes of cars starting with class A - Fiat Panda and Subaru Rex - both with 'On Demand Part-Time' systems followed by Subaru Justy in class B also with ODPT. In class C Toyota Tercel, Alfa 33, Subaru 1800, Mitsubishi Tredia, Mitsubishi Space Wagon and Honda Civic Shuttle all have on demand part-time systems, Volkswagen Golf Synchro is the only one in that class with Automatic Part-Time system. The offerings in class C/D are also impressive with VW Variant, Audi 80, Audi 90 and Ford Sierra all with 'COnstant' 4WD systems and finally also in the class C/D Renault 18 with on demand part-time system.

In the higher classes D and G the field of 4WD models thins out somewhat and in class D Audi

100, BMW 325i and Ford Scorpio are offered with constant 4WD system in addition to the American Motors Eagle with on demand part-time system. In class E Audi 200 and DB 300 TE are offered with constant 4WD, and finally in class G Audi Quattro with constant 4WD and the recently introduced Subaru XT with on demand part-time system and Porsche 959 with AUtomatic Part- Time are available.

Before the end of the 80's we expect 18 further 4WD models to enter the market, of which the majority will be from European car producers. In class A we are not aware of any 4WD entries emerging, but in class B two models are expected, one with on demand part-time system and the other with automatic part-time system. In class C we expect four models to appear in the market with a mixture of automatic part-time and constant systems. In class C/D two models are expected, both with automatic part-time systems. In class D two major models are expected, both with constant 4WD systems. The big onslaught is expected in class E with six major models of which five will be with constant 4WD system and one with automatic part-time system. Finally, in the sports car class G, two models are expected, one of which will have on demand part-time system and the other with automatic part-time system.

Consequently, at the beginning of the 90's there will be more than 40 different models in the market and the fact cannot be excluded that there could well then be some additional surprises in the market, particularly from Japanese producers, thus preparing for a rapid market development in the early 90's.

FORECAST OF FUTURE COMPETITIVE SITUATION IN WEST EUROPEAN CAR CLASSES - 1994

(FIG 6)

The expected rapid 4WD market development in Western Europe in the late 80's and early 90's will be stimulated and sustained by the increasing number of 4WD offerings. Our forecast of the model-volumes for 2WD cars with 4WD option in 1994 is shown in Fig 6. On the abscissa, the various car classes are indicated and on the ordinate, the number of cars in million units. Our forecast for the total number of cars in each car class in 1994 is an estimate based on available information from two independent automotive forecasting institutes. We are expecting a total market volume in class A of 0.6 million cars, in class B of 2.5 million cars, in class C of 3.4 million cars, in class C/D of 2 million cars, in class D of 1 million cars, in class E of 0.6 million cars and in the sports class G of 0.2 million cars.

In class A, the Fiat Panda market volume is substantial and we expect that 40% of the model-volume of the 2WD cars in this class will be offered with a 4WD option in 1994. The present 4WD development in class B is limited, but is expected to progress rapidly with emerging low cost 4WD systems. 40% of the model-volume of the 2WD coars in class B is expected to be offered with a 4WD option in 1994.

The large offering of 4WD models in class C is expected to be enhanced by additional models during the next few years and 50% of the model-volume in this class is expected to be 2WD cars with a 4WD option in 1994. In class C/D 60% of the model-volume is expected to be 2WD cars with a 4WD option. Corresponding figures for class D are 50% and for class E 40% and for class G, 5%.

As an average approximately 50% of the model-volume of all cars marketed in 1994 is expected to be 2WD cars with a 4WD option.

FORECAST OF FUTURE COMPETITIVE SITUATION IN WEST EUROPEAN MARKETS IN 1994

(FIG 7)

The total market-volume has in Fig 7 been applied to major market areas in Western Europe not, however, including Spain in view of the difficulties in forecasting that market. The Scandinavian (SCAN) market including Sweden, Norway, Finland and Denmark is expected to be 0.6 million cars, Belgium and Netherlands (BENE) 0.9 million cars, Germany (D) 2.5 million cars, Great Britain plus Ireland (GB + IRL) 1.9 million cars, France 2 million cars, Switzerland 0.28 million cars, Austria 0.27 million cars and Italy 1.7 million cars.

The 4WD offerings will differ quite substantially between the various market areas. In 1994 we expect that in West Germany - the biggest single market in Western Europe - 65% of the model-volume will be 2WD cars with a 4WD option. Switzerland and Austria are both expected to have a 51% model-volume of 2WD cars with a 4WD option. Great Britain and Ireland are expected to be at 48%, France at 38%, Italy at 34%, Benelux at 37% and Scandinavia at 32% model-volume of 2WD cars with a 4WD option in 1994.

The expected high number of 4WD offerings in West Germany, UK and France is to be attributed to the competitive situation in these markets including strong Japanese competition, particularly in the 4WD area, as well as to the concentration of the production in these countries. The customer acceptance of the 4WD penetration is a different question and will be analysed later in this paper. The high 4WD offering in Switzerland and Austria is due to the particular climatic and topographic conditions in these countries. The relatively low 4WD offering in the Scandinavian countries is due to the limited interest so far for 4WD solutions from the domestic car producers. The fairly low figure for Italy 34% is on account of the limited number of 4WD models expected to be offered from the Italian producers, as well as to their dominating position in the Italian market. The limited imports from non-EC countries are also contributing to keep 4WD offerings down. We further only consider the Northern Italian market to be a 4WD market.

FORECAST OF FUTURE 4WD PENETRATION IN WEST EUROPEAN MARKETS - 1994

(FIG 8)

We expect that the 4WD market penetration in Europe will be unevenly distributed due to differences in buying power, in climatic conditions and in topography.

In our opinion a dramatic development will take place in Switzerland from 6% of 4WD all conditions passenger cars in 1984 to 25% in 1994. The total 4WD penetration including Jeep-type vehicles in Switzerland in 1984 was approximately 8%. The 4WD penetration of all conditions passenger cars in Austria amounted in 1984 to 2.6% and is expected to increase to 12% in 1994. The overall 4WD penetration including Jeeps amounted to 4% in 1984.

A 4WD market penetration of 10% in Sweden relative to 0.7% in 1984 is anticipated. The 4WD Jeep penetration is Sweden is almost negligible. In Norway the 4WD penetration of all conditions passenger cars was zero %, but in 1994 is expected to be at the same level as in Sweden, i.e. 10%. Only Jeep-type vehicles were sold in Norway in 1984 and amounted to 1.5% of total car sales. The climatic conditions and the topography should make Norway a logical market for 4WD vehicles. We also expect a 10% 4WD market penetration in Finland by 1994, since the severe winter conditions will most likely stimulate the demand for 4WD cars.

In West Germany the 4WD all conditions penetration was 0.9% in 1984 (total 4WD penetration including Jeep-type vehicles 2.0%) and in 1994 we anticipate the 4WD all conditions penetration to be 7%.

A far lower 4WD all conditions penetration is expected in France with 4% in 1994 from only 0.2% in 1984. Total 4WD penetration, including Jeep-type vehicles amounted in 1984 to 0.5%. In Denmark we expect a 4WD penetration of all conditions cars of 3.5% in 1994, from only 0.2% in 1984.

Total 4WD penetration including Jeeps amounted to 0.3%. In UK the 4WD all conditions penetration amounted to 0.4% (all 4WD cars including Jeep-type vehicles to 0.8%) and the 4WD all conditions penetration is expected to be 3% in 1994.

In Italy the 4WD all conditions penetration amounted to 0.7% (total 4WD penetration including Jeep-type vehicles 1.2%) and we expect a 4WD all conditions penetration of 2.5% in 1994. We anticipate that the major part of this penetration will be centered around Northern Italy. Low penetration rates are expected in Belgium with 2%, in Netherlands 1.5% and in Ireland with 1.5% in 1994.

The buying power, topography and climatic conditions in the European Alpine areas as well as the Nordic countries would constitute the prime future 4WD market areas.

CONCLUSIONS

The prerequisites for a rapid development of the 4WD markets are low cost 4WD systems with improved vehicle dynamics characteristics and with a price compatibility for the mid- and downscale car market.

In 1994 we expect that approximately 70% of total Western World car production will be based on a car design incorporating transverse engine and front-wheel drive. Low cost 4WD systems for transverse engine cars must comply with strict NVH requirements and be compatible with applied anti-skid systems.

To some visionaries, our assessment of the 4WD
may seem too cautious and particularly so to
those, who in their crystal ball, already fore-
saw all cars with 4WD at the turn of the century.

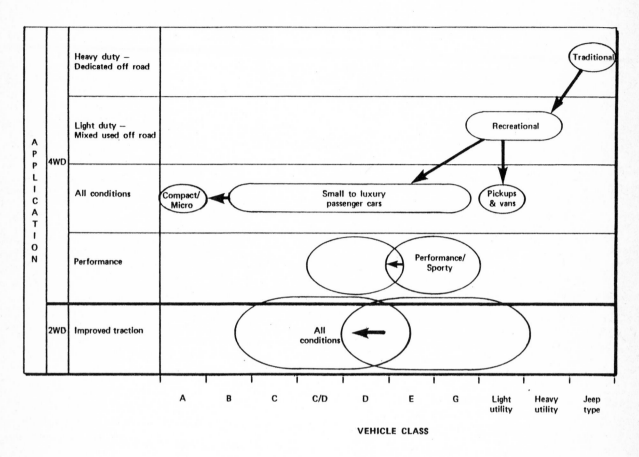

Fig 1   Application segments — four-wheel drive trends

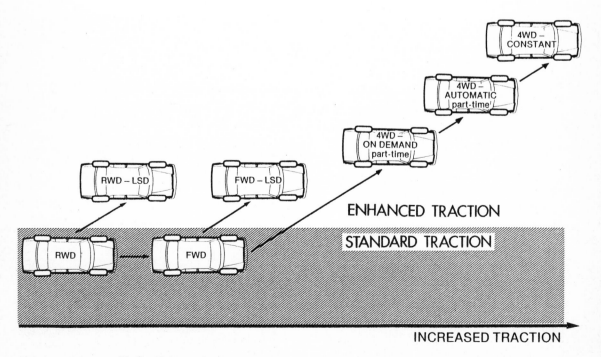

Fig 2   Enhanced traction systems — an attempt to categorize systems
for improved traction of 'all conditions' passenger cars

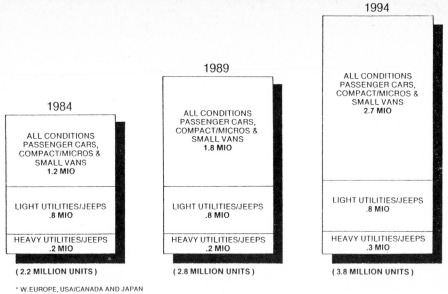

1984

ALL CONDITIONS
PASSENGER CARS,
COMPACT/MICROS &
SMALL VANS
1.2 MIO

LIGHT UTILITIES/JEEPS
.8 MIO

HEAVY UTILITIES/JEEPS
.2 MIO

(2.2 MILLION UNITS)

1989

ALL CONDITIONS
PASSENGER CARS,
COMPACT/MICROS &
SMALL VANS
1.8 MIO

LIGHT UTILITIES/JEEPS
.8 MIO

HEAVY UTILITIES/JEEPS
.2 MIO

(2.8 MILLION UNITS)

1994

ALL CONDITIONS
PASSENGER CARS,
COMPACT/MICROS &
SMALL VANS
2.7 MIO

LIGHT UTILITIES/JEEPS
.8 MIO

HEAVY UTILITIES/JEEPS
.3 MIO

(3.8 MILLION UNITS)

* W.EUROPE, USA/CANADA AND JAPAN

Fig 3   Forecast growth of annual world four-wheel drive production
         1984—94 by vehicle segments

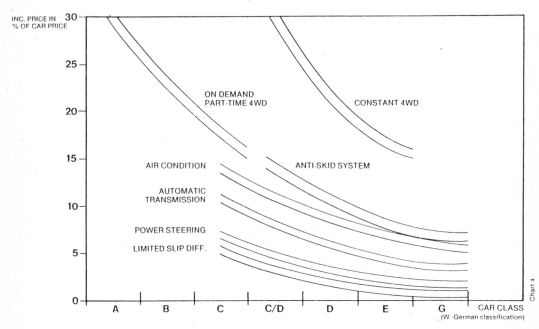

Fig 4   Price compatibility of options

		A	B	C	C/D	D	E	G	TOTAL
A P P L I C A T I O N	Introduced 4WD Models	● Fiat Panda (ODPT) ● Subaru Rex (ODPT)	● Subaru Justy (ODPT)	● Toyota Tercel (ODPT) ● Alfa 33 (ODPT) ● Subaru 1800 (ODPT) ● Mitsubishi-Tredia (ODPT) Space Wagon (ODPT) ● Honda Civic Shuttle (ODPT) ● VW Golf Syncro (AUPT)	● R18 (ODPT) ● VW Variant (CO) ● Audi 80 (CO) ● Audi 90 (CO) ● Ford Sierra (CO)	● Eagle (ODPT) ● Audi 100 (CO) ● BMW 325i (CO) ● Ford Scorpio (CO)	● Audi 200 (CO) ● DB 300 TE (AUPT)	● Audi Quattro (CO) ● Subaru XT (ODPT) ● Porsche 959 (AUPT)	24 models on the market
	Expected 4WD Models		2 models 1 ODPT 1 AUPT	4 models 3 AUPT 1 CO	2 models both AUPT	2 models both CO	6 models 5 CO 1 AUPT	2 models 1 AUPT 1 ODPT	18 models expected to enter the market during the next 5 years

Fig 5   Four-wheel drive entries in the market

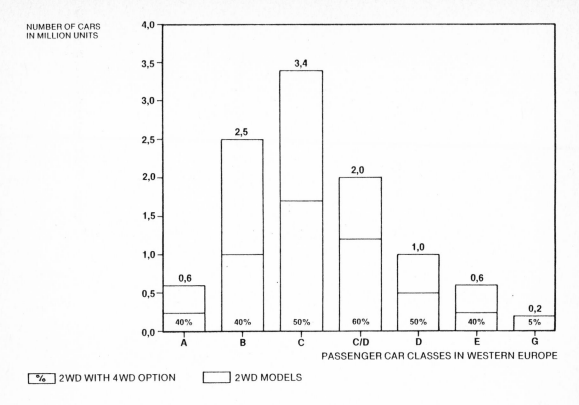

NUMBER OF CARS
IN MILLION UNITS

PASSENGER CAR CLASSES IN WESTERN EUROPE

[%] 2WD WITH 4WD OPTION   [ ] 2WD MODELS

Fig 6   Forecast of future competitive situation in West European car
        classes in 1994

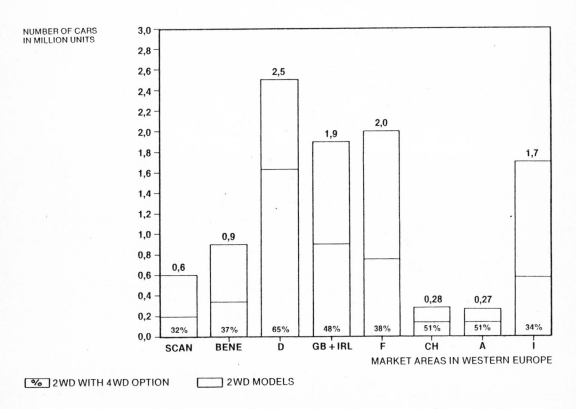

NUMBER OF CARS
IN MILLION UNITS

MARKET AREAS IN WESTERN EUROPE

[%] 2WD WITH 4WD OPTION   [ ] 2WD MODELS

Fig 7   Forecast of future competitive situation in West European markets
        in 1994

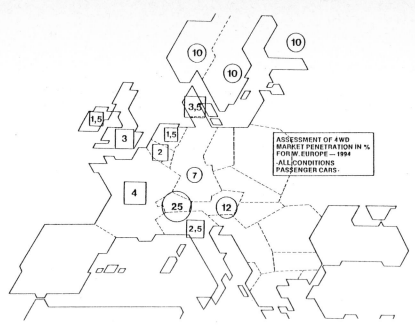

Fig 8   Forecast of future competitive situation in West European markets in
1994

Table 1   Car classification by marketing systems (West Germany)

CAR-CLASSES		TYPICAL CAR MODELS
Micro	A	Citroen 2CV, Citroen LNA, Renault 4, Fiat Panda, Daihatsu Cuore, Suzuki Alto, Subaru SA 310, Honda City
Mini	B	VW Polo, Ford Fiesta, Opel Corsa, Citroen Visa, Peugeot 104, Peugeot 205, Renault 5, Talbot Samba, ARNA, Fiat Uno, Lancia Y10, Autobianchi A 112, BL Metro, Toyota Starlet, Honda Civic, Nissan Micra, Nissan Cherry
Lower/Medium	C	VW Golf, VW Jetta, Ford Escort, Ford Orion, Opel Kadett, Citroen GSA, Talbot Horizon, Renault 9, Renault 11, BL Maestro, Alfa 33, Fiat Ritmo, Nissan Sunny, Honda Accord, Honda Prelude, Honda Quintet, Mazda 323, Mitsubishi Colt, Toyota Corolla, Toyota Tercel
Medium	C/D	VW Passat, Audi 80, Ford Sierra, Opel Ascona, Peugeot 305, Renault 18, Talbot-Solara, Citroen BX, BL Montego, Fiat 131, Mazda 626, Toyota Carina/Celica, Volvo 340/343
Upper Medium		Audi 100, BMW-3er, Ford Granada/Scorpio, Mercedes W201, Opel Rekord, Peugeot 505, Lancia Beta, Renault 25, Fiat Argenta, Alfa Romeo 90, Mitsubishi Galant, Mazda 929, Saab 900
Large and Executive		BMW-5er, BMW-7er, Mercedes W124, W126, Opel Senator, Opel Monza, Citroen CX, Volvo 240/740/760, Audi 200 Saab 9000, Rover, Jaguar, Lancia Thema
Sports cars	G	Porsche, Ferrari, Maserati, Audi Quattro, BMW-6er, D. Benz 107, Opel Manta, VW Scirocco, Renault Fuego, Alfa Alfetta GTV, Mazda RX7, Nissan 280 ZX, Subaru XT, Toyota MR2, Mitsubishi Cordia/Starion

Four-wheel drive vehicle dynamics computer simulation

H MINABE, BEng, T HASHIMOTO, BEng and M YAMANOTO, MEng
Toyota Motor Corporation, Aichi-Ken, Japan

SYNOPSIS   A 4WD simulation model was developed and an analysis made of the effects of front/rear torque distribution, centre differential lock-up and viscous coupling torque on disturbance response, loss of cornering stability, controllability of power oversteer and steerability when braking.

1 INTRODUCTION

4WD vehicles have long been used for military, agricultural and leisure purposes, but it is only relatively recently that 4WD systems have been applied to on-road passenger cars. Perhaps because of this, the concepts adopted are widely varied: part-time 4WD based on FWD or RWD; full-time 4WD with a centre differential, some giving equal front/rear torque distribution, others biased torque distribution, and 4WD deriving from device which varies the proportion of torque directed to the front and rear axles. As a consequence, handling charecteristics differ considerably from vehicle to vehicle. The traction, braking and steady-state cornering ability of 4WD as compared to 2WD is already fairly well documented (1) (2), (3) and recent research (4) has centred on the effects of 4WD variables on the afore-mentioned vehicle dynamics.

The purpose of this paper is to present a simulation model and analyze the way in which front/rear torque distribution, differential lock-up, and viscous coupling torque affect disturbance response, loss of cornering adhesion, controllability of power oversteer and steerability when braking.

2 SIMULATION MODEL

The simulation model, consisting of a vehicle body and power train as shown in Fig 1, has been kept fairly simple in view of the number of parameters involved in this study.

2.1 Vehicle body model

The model has four degrees of freedom: longitudinal velocity, lateral velocity, yaw angle and roll angle. Although it does not have pitch angle freedom, provision is made for front/rear weight distribution transfer when acceleration and braking is considered. The compliance steer by longitudinal force is set at zero. The compliance steer by lateral force and roll steer are expressed as co-efficients. Roll stiffness is proportional to roll angle and roll velocity. Front/rear distribution of roll stiffness matches that of the typical family car.

2.2 Power train model

The power train has five inertia momentums (engine/transmission and wheels/axles) connected through the front, centre and rear differentials. The transmission is manual and the clutch is engaged. If no differential is locked, there are four degrees of rotational freedom, but locking any differential reduces the number of degrees of rotational freedom. Consequently equations of motion were set up for the eight combinations possible. Two provisions are made for front/rear torque distribution:a geared centre differential and a viscous coupling device. Viscous coupling properties are simplified as shown in Fig 2a.

2.3 Vehicle data

The vehicle data is given below. The braking torque distribution is set up as defined in Fig 2b to represent that of a typical family saloon.

Vehicle mass	1450kg
Wheel base	2.6m
Tread (Front/Rear)	1.47/1.44m
Centre of gravity	0.525m
Moment of inertia (Z-Axis)	2600kgm^2
Moment of inertia (X-Axis)	520kgm^2
Weight distribution	57:43
Transmission gear ratio (1st/2nd/3rd/4th)	3.5/2.0/1.3/1.0
Final gear ratio	4.0

2.4 Tyre properties and road surfaces

Tyre traction force and side force are defined in slip-rate slip-angle maps. Properties are based on published reports (5) (6). To simplify the data-base,only the data corresponding to a tarmac road surface (Fig 2c) were programmed into the computer, maps corresponding to other surfaces (e.g gravel, snow, ice) being obtained by multiplication by the appropriate coefficient of friction.

3 SIMULATION RESULTS

3.1 Lateral force disturbance response.

The vehicle was assumed to be running along a straight road having a surface friction coefficient of 0.4 in second gear and to be generating 120 Nm engine torque. Random lateral forces with normal distribution (standard deviation=200N) were acting independently on the four wheels.

(a) Geared centre differential.

Four torque distribution ratios, 100:0(FWD), 60:40, 40:60 ,0:100(RWD) and differential lock-up were simulated and the respective yaw velocity root mean squares calculated. Fig 3a shows the calculated values. For purposes of

comparison the values measured on a test vehicle are also given. It will be noted that both sets of results show a similar pattern: the values become progressively lower as the torque distribution ratios approach that of centre differential lock-up. The reason for this lies in the fact that when the traction force is distributed to both front and rear tyres, the excess cornering force becomes greater (1). It therefore follows that the lowest value will result when torque distribution is equivalent to dynamic weight distribution, which is the case when the centre differential is locked. Although the simulated yaw velocity is very high in RWD, the measured value is considerably lower as the driver made steering corrections.
(b) Viscous coupling.
Coupling torque of 100Nm and 200Nm was applied to both FWD and RWD based 4WD systems. The results are given in Fig 3b. It was found that the value of the yaw velocity root mean square decreased in both cases as the coupling torque was increased. In other words, the stiffer the coupling, the closer the effective front/rear torque distribution ratios becomes to that of the dynamic weight distribution.

3.2 Longitudinal force disturbance response.
Simulations were made for a vehicle being driven in third gear at 50km/h along a straight road with a surface friction coefficient of 0.5. A random rearward longitudinal force with normal distribution (standard deviation= 1000Nm) was acting independently on each wheel at the point of contact with the road surface. Four levels of engine torque (-50Nm, 0Nm, 50Nm, 100Nm) were applied to FWD, RWD and 4WD based on a geared centre differential. Torque distribution was 50:50, and three differential lock-up/operating combinations were considered: centre differential operating, centre differential locked, centre and rear differentials locked. Fig 4 shows that at each level of engine torque, the lowest yaw velocity root mean square corresponds to the case of centre differential lock-up. The reason for this may be explained by the mechanical properties of the differentials. Assuming that a rearward disturbance force is acting on the leftside rear wheel, it will induce an anticlockwise yaw moment. If the centre differential is locked, the engine/transmission inertia prevents absorption of the force by the rear propeller shaft and consequently, due to the action of the rear differential, the force induces a counter rotation in the rightside rear wheel, which in turn induces a clockwise yaw moment that counters the initial anticlockwise yaw moment, thereby decreasing yaw velocity. If the centre differential is operating, a countering yaw moment will not occur. In the case of FWD and RWD, a countering yaw moment will occur if the rearward disturbance force is acting on either of the driven wheels, but will not occur if it is acting on one of the free wheels. If both centre and rear differentials are locked, a rearward force acting on either rear wheel will also act directly on the other rear wheel, thereby increasing yaw velocity.

3.3 Adhesion loss while cornering under power.
It was assumed that a vehicle which was accelerating round a bend in a road with surface friction coefficient 0.8 suddenly encountered a patch of ice (friction coefficient 0.2) ten metres long. The vehicle was in second gear,

the initial velocity was 36km/h; front tyre steer angle was 5°; and 100Nm engine torque acceleration was being applied.
(a) Geared centre differential.
Yaw velocity time histories were determined for torque distribution ratios of 0:100, 40:60, 60:40, 100:0 and for centre differential lock-up.
As can be seen in Fig 5a, yaw velocity changes at four points in time, i.e. front wheels onto the ice, rear wheels onto the ice, front wheels off the ice and rear wheels off the ice. RWD yaw velocity increases greatly when the rear wheels cross onto the ice, causing the vehicle to spin. On the other hand, FWD yaw velocity decreases while the front wheels are on the ice, inducing vehicle drift-out. With the centre differential operating, 4WD behaviour is similar to either RWD or FWD according to the torque distribution. When the centre differential is locked, the torque distribution is equal to the distribution of the product of the friction coefficient and dynamic weight. In this case the yaw velocity is very close to that of 60:40 torque distribution. To confirm these predictions, a test vehicle was operated under the conditions given above and yaw velocities measured for the same four torque distribution ratios. The measured results given in Fig 5b show good agreement with the simulations.
(b) Viscous coupling
Fig 5c shows the results for 4WD based on FWD and RWD. Coupling torque of 100Nm and 200Nm was applied. In either case, when the stiffer coupling is adopted, the yaw velocity time history approaches that of centre differential lock-up.

3.4 Power oversteer controllability
When deliberately induced power oversteer is used, vehicle controllability will depend on the inward angular velocity. If it is too fast or too slow, vehicle control is more difficult.
For the purpose of this investigation, the friction coefficient between the road surface and tyres is assumed to be 0.4. The vehicle is cornering at an initial speed of 36km/h in second gear, the front tyre steer angle being 10°, when engine torque is applied. (An engine torque curve typical of a family saloon was selected). The throttle is fully open in 0.2 sec.
(a) Geared centre differential
Yaw velocity time histories were calculated for centre differential lock up and four torque distribution ratios (0:100,40:60,60:40,100:0). The results are given in Fig 6a. Upon application of engine torque, RWD yaw velocity rises rapidly and the vehicle immediately spins in, whereas FWD yaw velocity decreases and the vehicle drifts out. In the case of 40:60 torque distribution there is a gentle increase in yaw velocity. If the centre differential is locked or torque distribution is 60:40, yaw velocity slightly decreases. The results are similar for the reasons given in 3.3 above. Fig 6b gives the time (in sec.) required to reach a body slip angle of 5°. From this figure it can be seen that sec. to 5° body slip increases as the proportion of torque applied to the rear wheels decreases. In the case of FWD, a body slip angle of 5° cannot be attained.
(b) Viscous coupling.
For this simulation, the base vehicles to which viscous coupling was added were a RWD and a 4WD with 40:60 geared torque distribution. It will

be observed from the yaw velocity curves (Fig 6c) that adding viscous coupling to either base vehicle shifts the curve towards that of centre differentiail lock-up, the shift becoming more pronounced with the higher torque coupling (200Nm). Fig 6d (sec.to 5° body slip) shows a similar increase. These findings indicate that the effect of viscous coupling is to weaken power oversteer.

(C) Effect of engine torque.
Power oversteer controllability is also affected by engine torque. Fig 6e shows sec. to 5° body slip when constant engine torque is applied. In the case of RWD, less than 0.5 sec. is required even at fairly low engine torque. As front torque distribution is increased, progressively greater engine torque is necessary for this rate to be attained. In other words, power oversteer can be controlled at the higher engine torque needed for fast acceleration.

3.5 Steerability during braking
It is sometimes necessary to steer while braking, but yaw velocity induced by steering is reduced by the braking force. In the simulation, the vehicle is running at 64km/h along a straight road having a surface friction coefficient of 0.8. Braking torque is applied and the steer angle set at 5°. The clutch remains engaged.

(a) Geared centre differential
Fig 7a shows yaw velocity time histories given that braking torque is 2800Nm. Yaw velocity is maintained if the centre differential is locked, but is diminished in all other cases, the diminution becoming greater as the front/rear torque distribution is shifted to the rear wheels. Fig 7b shows the maximum yaw velocities at various levels of braking torque. From this figure the maximum yaw velocities can be placed in the following order: centre differential lock-up FWD centre differental operating RWD (always assuming that the braking torque distribution as defined in Fig 2b applies). In the case of FWD, the power train inertia must be added to the inertia of the front wheel. Therefore during braking, the front braking torque is reduced by the total inertia, while the rear braking torque retains its full value. In the case of RWD, braking torque loss occurs at the rear. If the centre differential is operating, the distribution of true braking force (i.e. friction between tyre and road surface) will be intermediate to the distributions corresponding to FWD and RWD. However if the centre differential is locked, the distribution of true braking force will be better than that of FWD because the latter is less rear-biased. For this reason it has been said that when the centre differential is locked, the true braking distribution is ideal.

(b) Viscous coupling.
The base vehicles were FWD, RWD and a 4WD with 50:50 geared torque distribution. As indicated in Fig 7c viscous coupling increases the yaw velocity during braking. In all cases, when the higher torque coupling is applied, the true braking force distribution approaches that attained when the centre differential is locked.

4 CONCLUSION
A simulation model was developed to study 4WD handling characteristics resulting from two concepts: geared centre differential and viscous conpling device. Based on simulated results an analysis was made of the effects of front/rear torque distribution, differential lock-up and viscous coupling torque on disturbance response, cornering stability, and steerability during braking. Simulated results were compared to measured results obtained using a test vehicle and good agreement was found. The simulation model should therefore prove a useful aid to manufacturers of full-time 4WD vehicles in determining the concept and the gearing/coupling torque which will produce the characteristics best suited to the proposed vehicle.

References

1. Auditorium "Permanent four-wheel drive" in the Research and Development Centre, AUDI NSU AUTO UNION AG, Ingolstadt April,1984

2. Matumoto,R. Increase of driving Safely Through New Concept 4WD Vehicle. 9th ESV International Conference

3. Obayashi,S. Kobayashi,Y. Takahashi,A. Characteristics of Manoeuvrability of 4WD Vehicle. Journal of SAE Japan vol.39 No.3 1985

4. Flegl,H. Foldi,Th. and Witte,L. Handling Characteristics of Four-wheel Drive Vehicles. 8th IAVSD Symposium Aug.1983

5. Sakai,H Research on the Dynamic Properties of Tire. Japan Automobile Research Institute Technical Report No.46 April,1978

6. Bernard,J.E. Segel,L. and Wild,R.E. Tire shear Force Generation During Combined Steering and Braking Maneuvers. SAE Paper 770852

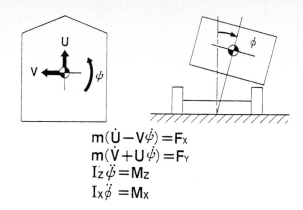

$$m(\dot{U}-V\dot{\psi})=F_X$$
$$m(\dot{V}+U\dot{\psi})=F_Y$$
$$I_Z\ddot{\psi}=M_Z$$
$$I_X\ddot{\phi}=M_X$$

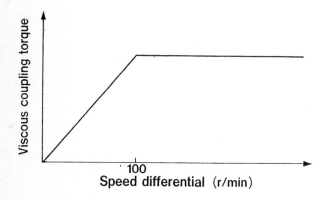

$$\begin{pmatrix} \text{Inertia} \\ \\ \text{matrix} \end{pmatrix} \times \begin{pmatrix} \dot{\omega}_1 \\ \dot{\omega}_2 \\ \dot{\omega}_3 \\ \dot{\omega}_4 \end{pmatrix} = \begin{pmatrix} \text{Torque} \\ \\ \text{vector} \end{pmatrix}$$

Fig 1 Simulation model

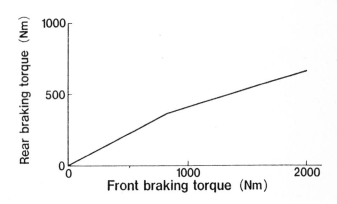

Fig 2a Viscous coupling

Fig 2b Braking torque distribution

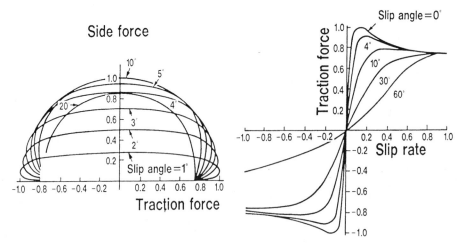

Fig 2c Tyre properties

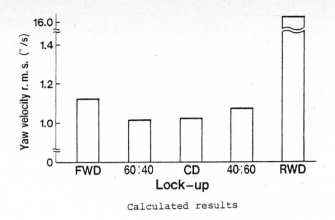

Calculated results

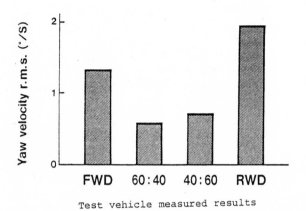

Test vehicle measured results

Fig 3a Yaw velocity root mean squares (geared centre differential)

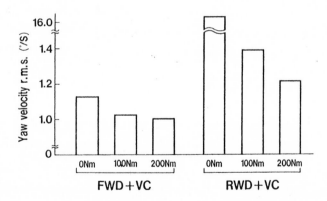

Fig 3b Yaw velocity root mean squares (viscous coupling)

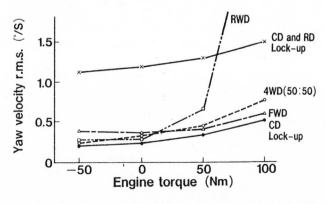

Fig 4 Yaw velocity root mean squares induced by longitudinal force

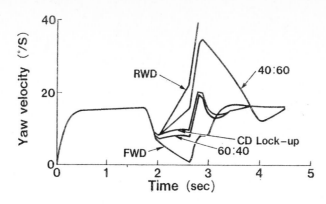

Fig 5a Adhesion loss while cornering (geared centre differential) —
simulation results

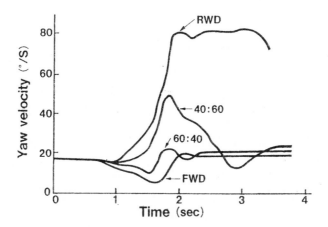

Fig 5b Adhesion loss while cornering (geared centre differential) —
measured results

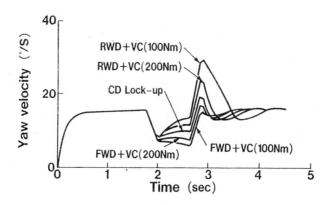

Fig 5c Adhesion loss while cornering (viscous coupling)

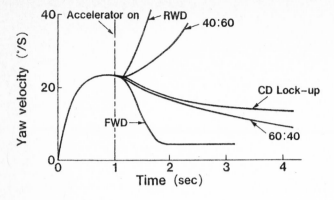

Fig 6a Yaw velocity (geared centre differential)

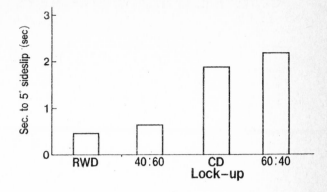

Fig 6b Second to 5° body slip angle (geared centre differential)

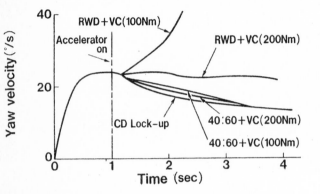

Fig 6c Yaw velocity (viscous coupling)

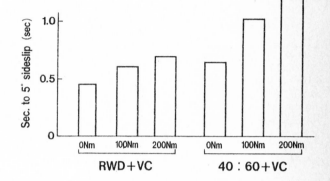

Fig 6d Second to 5° body slip angle (viscous coupling)

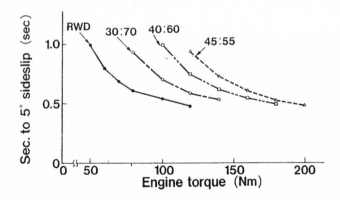

Fig 6e Second to 5° body slip angle (geared centre differential)

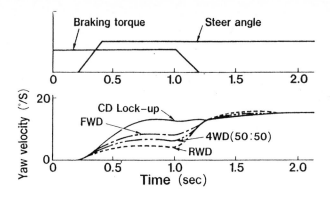

Fig 7a Steerability during braking

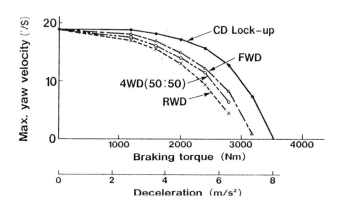

Fig 7b Maximum yaw velocity during braking

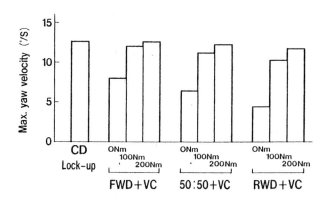

Fig 7c Steerability during braking (viscous coupling)

24

Historical survey of four-wheel drive

P FRÈRE
Venc, France

The Dutch Spyker company is better known for the fact it produced the first six-cylinder car for sale to the public, than for exhibiting the first car featuring a mechanical drive to all four wheels at the Paris Salon of 1903. It seems however, that it remained at the prototype stage and that the exhibit was not followed by production models. The layout devised by the Spyker brothers however led the way to be followed later by many other manufacturers, most of which specialised in off-road vehicles : based on a conventional front engine, rear wheel drive vehicle, its gearbox was extended laterally to an outrigger from which the propeller shaft driving the front wheels took its movement. As far as I could ascertain, the drive to the front wheels was non-permanent and could be selected by a dog clutch.

At the time, one of the big problems of four-wheel drive was the lack of homokinetic joints. Only Hooke joints existed and while they allowed steering the front wheels, the rotating movement transmitted to them was irregular - sinuosïdal in fact - and the amplitude of the speed (and torque) variations increased with an increasing lock. Forty-five years later, when homokinetic joints had long been invented and were currently available, Citroën used simple Hooke joints to drive the front wheels of the 2 CV, in an attempt to save cost. Those of us who have driven early 2 CVs cannot fail to remember the awful reactions which resulted in the steering, forcing the driver to declutch or at least slip the clutch as soon as a sharp bend had to be rounded.

A car which had neither this problem, nor the problem created by the speed differential of the front and rear wheels when rounding a bend was the "mixed drive" car designed by Ferdinand Porsche for his employer, the Lohner company in Vienna, and of which several models were built and sold between 1903 and 1907.

Porsche had joined Lohner in 1900 to build electric cars of which the motors were incor - porated into the front wheel hubs and as early as 1900 he built a four-wheel drive version, with a motor in each wheel, to the order of a certain E.W. Hart, in Luton, who wanted more performance for racing. The weight of its batteries alone was 1800 kg ! The weight of the batteries soon proved an unsurmountable handicap and from 1903 on, Porsche took out some patents on what he called the "mixed drive" : a petrol engine drove a dynamo which, in turn, fed the two front hub mounted direct current motors. These cars were more satisfactory but not fast enough for racing - and all his life Porsche was an addict of racing as a proving ground and an incentive to development. It is thus not surprising that he entered one of his cars, which he drove himself, for the Semmering Hill Climb which took place near Vienna in 1903, and to achieve the required performance, he used four hub mounted motors, one in each wheel. This Porsche-Lohner was probably the first four-wheel drive car powered by a petrol engine seen in an official competition. Due to the fact that there was no mechanical link between the four motors, the problem of speed differentials bet- ween the four wheels when cornering was entirely solved. It is worthy of note that it was old Ferdinand Porsche's grandson, Ferdinand Piëch, who really made four-wheel drive for road cars take off when he designed the Audi Quattro.

The next four-wheel drive car to hit the headlines was also a racing car, designed, built and driven by that great American pioneer Walter Christie who entered it for the Vanderbuilt Cup Race in 1905. In this case too, the four-wheel drive resulted from the quest for more power. In the previous year, Christie had made some successful record attempts with a car powered by a huge 13.4 litre, four-cylinder engine mounted transversally and driving the front wheels through a two-speed gearbox. For the Vanderbuilt Cup Race, he wanted more power and added a similar set-up, though of slightly smaller size, to the rear of his vehicle, driving the rear wheels. As the race was run on on oval with large radius curves, the lack of homokinetic joints was not a major handicap, but the car didn't do particularly well. It took 48 years for others to take up Christie's idea, when John Cooper and Daniel Richmond of Downton Engi- neering both built a twin engined Mini, neither of which was very successful. But in the late thirties, the principle of having the two sets of wheels driven independently by two engines (in this case mounted amidships, side by side) was successfully used in John Cobb's Land speed record beating car, designed by Reid Railton.

The United States was probably the first country where four wheel drive passenger cars were built in any number when a blacksmith called Otto Zachow and a certain William Besserdich started a car factory in Clintonville, Wisconsin, which, after producing some conventional cars, started adding front wheel drive around 1908. But they soon concentrated in applying their four-wheel drive system to commercial vehicles produced under the trade mark FWD. Their layout was conventional with optional drive to the front wheels from a transfer box outrigged from the gearbox. Many of these vehicles were used by the American forces during World War I and many could be seen in regular use many years after the war ended.

It would be too long to recall the four-wheel drive vehicles built for civil and military use from heavy tractors to the ubiquitous Jeep of World War II, almost all of which were conventional in their design, with an outrigged transfer box driving the front wheels at will. Probably the first which did not follow this standard practice was the military version of the VW Beetle which was produced as a scout car with the well-known saloon body and in amphibian version. As everyone knows, the standard "Beetle" had (and still has, as it is still being produced in Mexico and in Brasil) its flat-four engine overhung at the rear, from where the drive was taken forward to the gearbox, ahead of the rear wheel axis, and back to the final drive. With this layout, adding a drive to the front wheels is the easiest thing imaginable : all that is needed is a propeller shaft driven by a dog clutch from the free forward end of the gearbox output shaft and a bevel gear driven differential driving the front wheels, the dog clutch being engaged at the driver's will, when the going becomes difficult. This is certainly the simplest, cheapest, lightest and least power absorbing way of achieving four-wheel drive. In principle, it is the same layout as featured in the Audi Quattro, turned 180° , and in the four-wheel drive models made by Porsche.

In all the vehicles I have mentioned up to now, it was up to the driver to select the drive to the front wheels incase the going became difficult. But in the case of fast cars, it seems obvious that the merits of four-wheel drive should be exploited permanently and the current trend is towards permanent four-wheel drive. This implies that two basic requirements are fulfilled :
a) provision must be made to allow the front
   wheels to rotate faster than the rear wheels
   when the vehicle rounds a bend.

b) the front drive shafts must include homokinetic joints to allow the front wheels to be
   driven at a constant speed whatever the
   steering angle.

To the best of my knowledge, the first car with permanent four-wheel drive was the Type 53 Bugatti racing car of which three were built in 1931, when it was thought that rear drive only would not be able to transmit the torque produced by the supercharged 4.9 litre engine in the lower gears.

In this car which further departed from traditional Bugatti practice by featuring indenpendent front suspension, the gear driven output shaft was included in the main gearbox casing and offset to the left. It drove the rear propeller shaft directly, while the propshaft to the front wheels was driven through a bevel gear differential splitting the torque equally between the front and rear axles. Homokinetic joints consisting of two Hooke joints set end to end and offset by 90° were used at the wheel end of the front drive shafts.

This type 53 was reputed to be a difficult car to drive and this is the reason why it was used only for hill climbs in which it was fairly successful up to 1935. René Dreyfus who drove the car on several occasions told me that he never even attempted to get it into a drift and just relied on the excellent grip to accelerate out of tight bends. I would think that the main reason for the difficult handling of the car was the combination of a very high rear roll centre and a front roll centre at ground level, resulting in a much higher roll stiffness at the rear than at the front and consequent oversteer.

Four-wheel drive for road cars only became a practical proposition after front wheel drive had reached a satisfactory stage of development, itself dependent on the availability of homokinetic joints. To the best of my knowledge, these were first seen on a small German car designed by Richard Bussien, of which a few were built in Berlin in 1925-26. It was called a VORAN (standing for VORderrad ANtrieb -front wd) and to achieve the homokinetic drive to the front wheels, Bussien simply used two Hooke joints end to end, as Bugatti did a few years later. They were rather bulky and required a considerable wheel offset. Though not many Voran cars were sold, an experimental Voran bus was put into regular service in Berlin around 1929. It was made by the NAG company to which Bussien had moved and for which he later designed another front driven small car.

But the real breakthrough in homokinetic joints came with the Tracta and Rzeppa joints, patented around 1926-27. The former was invented by the French engineer Pierre Fenaille and improved by Jean-Albert Grégoire who was one of the most active promoters of front wheel drive and built the Tracta sports car which he drove himself at Le Mans and in other events to prove the worth of both his joints and front wheel drive. The Rzeppa joint was invented by the Czech engineer who gave the joint his name. In principle, they are based on a double Hooke joint, but both are much more compact. These two joints really made front wheel drive - and hence four-wheel drive - a practical proposition. Both were used almost exclusively in four-wheel drive military vehicles of both camps during World War II.

It was not before World War II ended however, that any interest was shown in four-wheel drive for road going passenger cars. For this application, permanent four-wheel drive is certainly the more attractive solution, especially in the case of high performances cars in which wheel spin limits the performance and creates handling problems on wet roads.

One of the first cars in which all four wheels were driven permanently was the T3 Rover turbine car designed by Spen King when he was in charge of gas turbine development at Rover. It had a rear-mounted engine and, as had been the case of four-wheel drive VW Beetles, the gearbox output shaft was extended forward to drive the front-wheels through a conventional propeller shaft. The novel feature was that the drive to the front wheels incorporated a free wheel which allowed them to overrun the rear wheels when the car rounded a bend. In this case, of course, no drive was transmitted to the front wheels as long as they ran faster than the rear ones, but as soon as the rear wheels started to spin, they caught up with the front wheels to split the torque over all four wheels.

Also in the early fifties, the Ferguson company became interested in four-wheel drive and developed its own system incorporating a differential splitting the torque of the gearbox output shaft between the front and rear axles, while allowing for the higher speed of the front wheels whenever the car is not driven in a straight line. A conventional bevel gear differential was used, splitting the torque equally between front and rear. Though with this system, the driving force put through each wheel is halved, compared with two-wheel drive, there is still a possibility that on very slippery ground, one set of wheels, or even a single wheel will, under extreme conditions, loose its grip, setting a limit to the torque directed to the set of wheels having a better grip. In the early Ferguson system, this was prevented by using two overrun clutches (free wheels) locking up the drive whenever one set of wheels started spinning, two overrun clutches being necessary to take care of either front or rear wheel spin. The system was completed by a mechanical Dunlop "Maxaret" anti-lock system. The latter effectively prevented the wheels from locking in a panic stop, but its action was too slow, and as it governed all four wheels simultaneously and operated on the "select low" principle, it reduced the fluid pressure in all four brake lines as soon as a single wheel started locking. This, in fact, resulted in increased stopping distances.

To demonstrate his system, Ferguson built several prototype cars, pioneering the layout later adopted by Audi, with the engine overhanging the front wheel axis and the gearbox output shaft, carrying the torque splitting differential, extended forward to drive the front wheels and driving a propeller shaft from its rear end. The car was widely demonstrated to try and persuade the industry to adopt the design, but the car apparently came before its time. To more convincingly and publicly demonstrate the virtues of four-wheel drive, Ferguson then built a racing car, called "Project 99", to the specifications of the contemporary Formula One, using a 1.5 litre Coventry Climax engine. Its layout was more conventional with an inboard mounted front engine and an outrigger containing the differential from which propeller shafts drove the front and rear wheels. The Maxaret anti-lock brake control was not used. Driving this car, Stirling Moss just ran away from the opposition, most of them using an identical engine, in the rain soaked Gold Cup Race at Oulton Park in 1961 and would have won another event the same year, had he not been disqualified on a trivial matter. But the only manufacturer who took notice was Jensen for whom Harry Ferguson Research Ltd converted the Interceptor to four-wheel drive to make the Jensen FF. In this car, which was launched at the London Motor Show of 1967, the system had been taken one step further insofar as the torque splitting differential was now of epicyclic type, apporting 63% of the torque to the rear and 37% to the front wheels in order to reduce understeer and preserve the handling pattern of a rear wheel driven car. In addition, the mechanical anti-lock control was replaced by an electronic one, though still of the select low type.

A major simplification of the Ferguson system came with the replacement of the two overrun clutches by a single viscous coupling leaving the torque splitting differential virtually free for small differences in the rotating speed of the front and rear wheels, as when cornering, but progressively and effectively locking the differential solid when the speed differential increases, as happens when one set of wheels begins to spin. The viscous coupling saves weight and a lot of space and this has made the Ferguson system adaptable also to cars with a front mounted transverse engine, where the drive to the rear wheels implies the use of bevel gears and space is at a premium.

In the 'seventies, many cars were converted to four-wheel drive by FF Developments Ltd. for special purposes, many of them for the police, but it took another decade before major manufacturers became really interested in the Ferguson system which is now used by such manufacturers as Ford, BMW and Peugeot who uses the system for his immensely successful 205 Turbo 16 Rally car.

In the late sixties, several Formula One teams became interested in four-wheel drive, as the tyre manufacturers had failed to keep up with the sudden power increase brought about by the Ford-Cosworth DFV engine. Such cars were built by BRM Matra, Lotus, McLaren and Cosworth, but only BRM Matra and Lotus actually ran their car. In all cases, an epicyclic torque splitting differential was used to transfer more torque to the rear than to the front wheels, which is logical in view of the rear weight bias of those cars in which the engine was located behind the cockpit, a bias increased by the weight transfer under a Grand Prix car's fierce acceleration. Of the cars actually raced, Matra used the Ferguson system while Lotus had not provided any means of limiting the slip of the central differential. As it turned out, the extra weight and insufficient development made up for the better grip provided and the cars were unlucky insofar as in 1968, the year in which they appeared, none of the races was run in wet conditions. In the following year, racing tyre technology had made such progress that all those projects were shelved. To-day, Formula One cars powered by turbocharged engines developing some 800 bhp would probably benefit from four-wheel drive, but current regulations specify two-wheel drive only.

What is not generally known, however is that, before adopting the Ferguson system, Matra had built an experimental car featuring hydrostatic drive to the front wheels. In this car, a gearbox driven high pressure pump fed oil to receivers mounted in the front wheel hubs, a by-pass connection allowing for the different speed of the front wheels when cornering. In the final version, the receivers would have been mounted inboard to reduce the unsprung weight, but development took more time than expected, which led to the adoption of the Ferguson system.

Whatever the merits of the pionners, there is no doubt that the car which triggered the four-wheel drive boom is the Audi Quattro. In itself an impressive 200 bhp car combining sports car performance with excellent comfort and remarkable safety, its 400 bhp rally version really started a new era in the rally sport and brought home the merits of four-wheel drive to a very large public. It is also a car of high technical merit, for its transmission is certainly the cleanest and lightest permanent four-wheel drive design imaginable. Driving the rear wheels from a gearbox just aft of the front wheel axis is the simplest thing imaginable. But it normally means that a dog clutch must be provided to disconnect the propeller shaft driving the rear wheels when the car is driven on metalled roads providing a good grip. If the drive is to be permanent, a differential is necessary and Audi solved the problem of getting the drive from this differential to the front final drive by making the gearbox output shaft hollow to accomodate the shaft carrying the front bevel gear. As the Quattro is a nose heavy car, a bevel gear central differential is used, splitting the torque equally between the front and rear drives, but an epicyclic differential providing an unequal torque split could be used if required. In the particular case of the Audi, the differential can be locked, but fitting a Ferguson viscous coupling would not be a problem.

What is probably the latest development in four-wheel drive systems is being used by Porsche in their new type 959, to be made in road going and racing versions. In this 450 bhp rear engined car of 911 derivation, of which the racing version will develop over 600 bhp, the drive to the front wheels is taken through a multiplate clutch engaged by hydraulic pressure adjusted manually, but with the provision of an electronic overriding control which alters the hydraulic pressure as a function of signals given by a

sensor registering acceleration and deceleration and consequent weight transfer. The idea is that the pressure acting on the clutch, which limits the torque transmitted to the front wheels, is to be adjusted by a manual control, according to the grip provided by the road surface : dry, wet, dirt, etc ... In addition, if any set of wheels begins to spin, the electronic control intervenes to readjust the hydraulic pressure to transfer more torque to the set of wheels having the better grip.

Much less sophisticated is the system to be found in the VW Golf "Syncro" which, basically, has front wheel drive, but in which the rear wheels are linked to the gearbox output shaft by a simple viscous coupling which transfers part of the driving torque to the rear wheels as the front wheels begin to spin and consequently a speed differential is created between front and rear wheels. In this vehicle, the basic characteristics of a front wheel drive vehicle are preserved in all normal driving conditions where front wheel grip is sufficient.

This, I believe, covers the most important steps of four-wheel drive from the beginning of this century to date. I have concentrated more on the principle layouts than on the actual installations, keeping the accent mostly on production touring cars and dismissing most of the competition models having their engine located centrally, which widely differ in the installation of the various units, but stick to the major principles of modern systems.

Fig 1

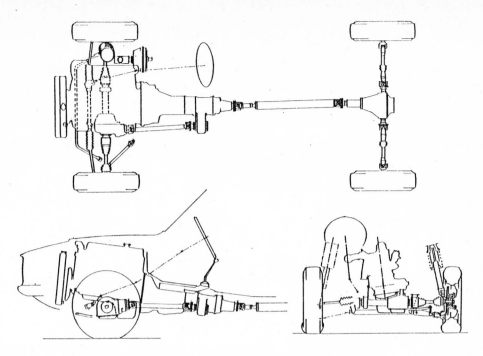

Fig 2   Typical four-wheel drive installation

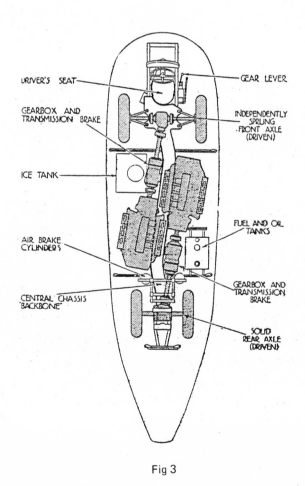

DRIVER'S SEAT

GEAR LEVER

GEARBOX AND
TRANSMISSION BRAKE

INDEPENDENTLY
SPRUNG
FRONT AXLE
(DRIVEN)

ICE TANK

FUEL AND OIL
TANKS

AIR BRAKE
CYLINDERS

GEARBOX AND
TRANSMISSION
BRAKE

CENTRAL CHASSIS
'BACKBONE'

SOLID
REAR AXLE
(DRIVEN)

Fig 3

1932 BUGATTI TYPE 53

Fig 4

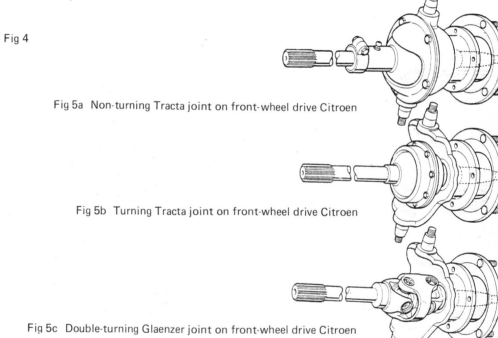

Fig 5a Non-turning Tracta joint on front-wheel drive Citroen

Fig 5b Turning Tracta joint on front-wheel drive Citroen

Fig 5c Double-turning Glaenzer joint on front-wheel drive Citroen

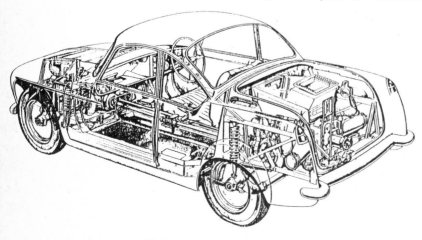

Fig 6

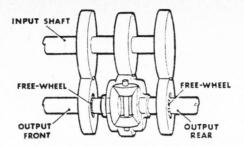

Fig 7   The basic principle (not the actual layout) of the Ferguson differential.
The drive is transmitted through the central gear set to the differential
cage: the other two gears on the two output shafts are driven at a
higher speed and idle on their free-wheels. But if either shaft
accelerates to the same speed as the gear revolving on it the free-wheel
locks and prevents any further increase

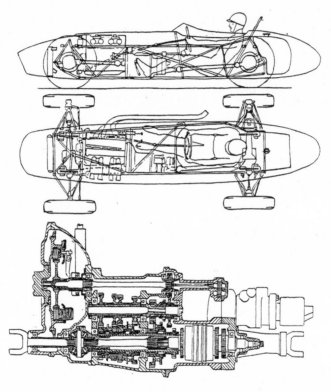

Fig 8

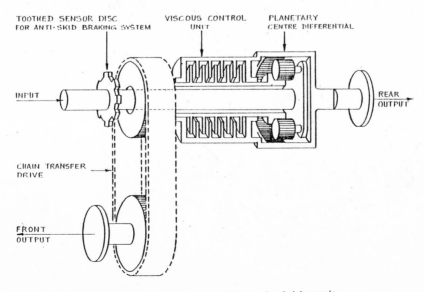

Fig 9   Diagrammatic layout of four-wheel drive unit

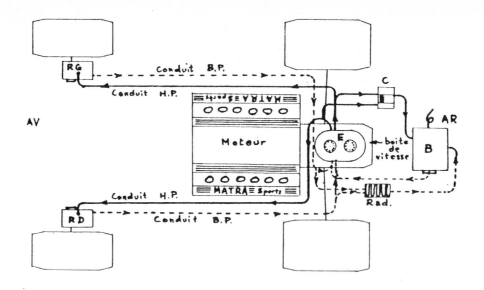

Fig 10 Principles and description of how the four-wheel drive unit works

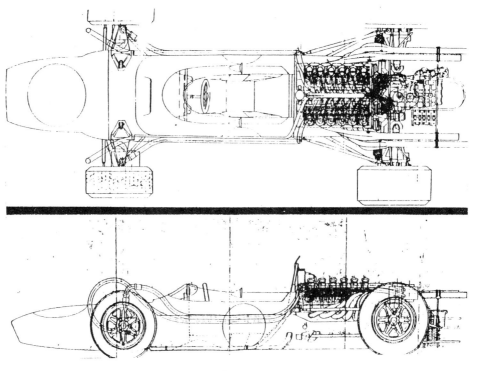

Fig 11

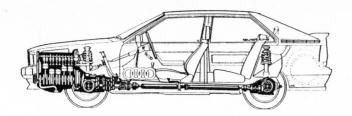

Fig 12

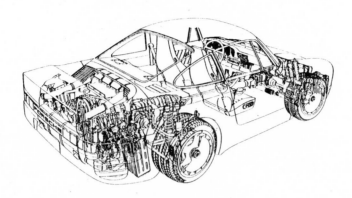

Fig 13 Porsche 959

Fig 14

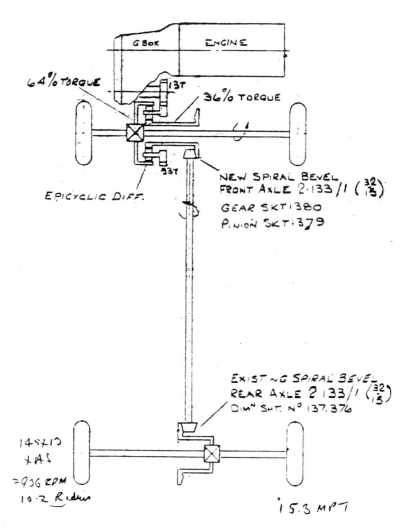

64% TORGUE

13T

36% TORQUE

EPICYCLIC DIFF.

33T

NEW SPIRAL BEVEL
FRONT AXLE 2·133/1 ($\frac{32}{15}$)

GEAR SKT·1380
PINION SKT·1379

EXISTING SPIRAL BEVEL
REAR AXLE 2·133/1 ($\frac{32}{15}$)
DIM^N SHT. N° 137.376

145×13
× AS

=936 RPM
10·2 Radius

15.3 MPT

Fig 15

34

© IMechE 1986 C02/86

Anti-skid brake system for four-wheel drive cars

H Y YUASA, MSc, M T TANI, PhD, T F FUNAKOSHI, MSc
Mitsubishi Motors Corporation, Okazaki, Aichi, Japan

SYNOPSIS   A simple two channel ASB system for 4WD cars with two sensors and two
diagonally connected brake line has shown almost similar improvement in braking
distance and directional stability as compared with a three channel ASB system for
2WD cars.

1   INTRODUCTION

Four wheel drive (4WD) cars generally
have   better   traction   and   cornering
performance   than two wheel drive (2WD)
cars by distributing traction forces to
all   four   wheels.   Furthermore,   before
wheel lock, 4WD cars have better braking
performance   under most of road adhesion
conditions   and   loading   conditions,
because each wheel is constrained through
the   drive line to rotate at the same
speed   and   generate   maximum   braking
forces simultaneously. However, once a
wheel   lock   occurs especially   under an
asymmetric road condition where a brake
force coefficient is different between
right and left sides of the vehicle, more
unstable behaviour will occur as compared
with a 2WD car.
In   order to prevent   this   unstable
behaviour,   the anti skid brake (ASB)
system is applied to 4WD cars, which
detects the condition causing any wheel
lock   and   controls the brake fluid
pressure to prevent a wheel lock. When a
four wheel ASB system for 2WD cars (three
channel ASB) is applied to 4WD cars,
aditional devices or more complicated
controls such as yaw cotrol are required,
because the drive line constraint causes
torque interferences among each wheel.
In   this paper, authors examined
feasibility of a two channel ASB system
for   4WD cars which utilizes   torque
transmitting characteristics among each
axles of 4WD cars.

2   BRAKING   CHARACTERISTICS   OF   2WD   AND   4WD CARS

2.1   State of wheel lock

There   are   several types of wheel lock,
from one wheel to all wheels, during a
brake application.   In the case of 2WD cars,
all types are likely to occur depending on
driving or road conditions. On the
other hand, the state of wheel lock of a
4WD car with its centre differential
locked is considered to be restricted
almost   to all wheel lock or two wheel
lock (one in an axle). Three wheel lock,
two front wheel lock or two rear wheel
lock will induce the deceleration of
rotation of the rest wheels and result in
immediate all wheel lock. Any single
wheel lock is also unlikely to occur due
to   interia of   three rotating   wheels
forcing the remaining wheel to rotate
through the drive line when driving force
is   higher than brake force. Usually
single   wheel   lock   also results   in
immediate all wheel lock.

2.2   Maximum brake force

Fig.1   shows general characteristics of
front and rear brake force distribution
for 2WD and 4WD cars (1). The term "4WD"
in   this paper means a 4WD car with its
centre differential locked. In case of
2WD cars, brake factors are designed to
give brake force distribution to prevent
unstable rear wheel lock. Therefore,
front brake force reaches the maximum
point   of brake force   coefficient curve
prior to the rear reaching the maximum.
A 4WD car is supposed to have the same
tire slip ratio among all wheels since
each   wheel tends to rotate at the same
speed due to the drive line constraint.
The brake torque is so transmitted from
front to rear through the drive line that
the   brake force distribution between
front and rear wheels is on the ideal
brake force curve as shown in Fig.1.
Therefore, front and rear wheels reach
the maximum braking force point (the
maximum   deceleration   point)
simultaneously. From this reason, 4WD
cars generally have a higher limit of
braking   force (deceleration) and shorter
braking distance than 2WD cars. Some
test rsults have shown that a 4WD car had
5 per cent higher deceleration and 5 per
cent shorter braking distance than a   2WD

car on a slippery road.

2.3 Directonal stability

In case of the brake operation during cornering, front wheels of a 2WD car tend to lock first causing lack of steerability. However, cornering force on the rear wheels still remains, and a car goes out of course with its direction nearly straight. Once braking force exceeds the level of any wheel lock in a 4WD car, the wheel lock induces other wheels to lock causing no steerability and spin of the car. Under a rather special condition such as an asymmetric road where a brake force coefficient is different between right and left sides of the vehicle, the wheel rotational speed of 2WD and 4WD cars during braking was observed as shown in Fig.2. Only one side of front wheels locked at the early stage of braking in case of a 2WD car. However, in case of a 4WD car, each one of front and rear wheels on the lower coefficient road side locked at the same time generating a larger turning moment as compared with that of a 2WD car. The rear wheel of a 2WD car on the higher coefficient road side was still rotating and generated cornering force even at the period after all wheels had locked in a 4WD car.

2.4 Mathematical simulation

Fig.3 shows the mathematical simulation model which is similar to the one developed by Flegl et al. (2) for analyzing the behaviour of 4WD cars. Tires and a drive line of a 4WD car were subdivided into 14 masses and 6 springs constituting the eleven-degrees-of-freedom model. Brake, traction, and cornering forces of tires were calculated by stress estimation of the deformation of a tire rubber block. The model has front, rear and centre differentials, and the characteristic of each differential has the variation of conventional differential, limited slip differential or locked differential. Brake characteristics were also included in the model.

Fig.2 shows the comparison between the test result and the calculation of wheel speeds of 4WD and 2WD cars on an asymmetric road. The calculated wheel speed showed generally good agreements with the test results. Large deviation of the calculated speed from the test result after 0.8 sec in case of a 2WD car was caused by poor calculation accuracy of dynamic weight transfer during vehicle rolling.

3 ANTI SKID BRAKE SYSTEM FOR 4WD CARS

3.1 ASB system

Fig.4 shows the schematic diagram of ASB systems tested, namely a two channel system, a single channel system for 4WD cars and a three channel system well known among 2WD cars (3) (4) (5).

ASB controls the tire slip ratio within the appropriate range in which both the brake efficiency and stability are guaranteed. An ASB system consists of wheel rotational speed sensors, an acceleration sensor and a control unit which calculates the tire slip ratio and decreases or increases brake fluid pressure. The acceleration sensor is used to calculate the vehicle speed change. When wheel speed sensors are used for the calculation of vehicle speed change in 4WD cars, the calculated result will be misleading because each wheel has the same speed change in most of braking situation, whereas a three channel system for 2WD cars uses wheel speed sensors for the speed change calculation.

Regarding wheel rotational speed sensors, each sensor on all wheels is necessary for a 2WD car because any single wheel lock will occur. In case of a 4WD car, the states of four wheel lock and two wheel lock each in front and rear will be detected by positioning two sensors at front or rear wheels. By positioning one sensor on the drive line, for example at the transfer shaft, the state of four wheel lock will be detected, while the position of locked wheels cannot be identified. Fig.5 shows the state of wheel lock possible to occur ignoring transient state in a 4WD car and the position of sensors equipped to detect each state.

In order to control the brake fluid pressure, two diagonal brake lines have been equipped with independent actuators. By this brake system, four wheel lock and diagonal two wheel lock shown in Fig.5 can be controlled completely. Furthermore, the case (a) of two wheel lock is also expected to be controlled because one of the locked wheels starts to rotate by reducing the corresponding brake line pressure and three rotating wheels force the remaining locked wheel to rotate as far as inertia force is larger than braking force. This behaviour of rotational speed recovery was observed in the vehicle running tests.

As for a single channel ASB system, all wheels are controlled together to prevent any wheel lock. When any wheel lock occurs, the brake fluid pressure of unlocked wheels are also reduced so that braking distance tends to be longer. In spite of this disadvantage, the dominant state of lock in a 4WD car is all wheels lock so that a single channel system is still expected to keep the stability of a car during brake operation, while lack of lateral control has been reported (6) in the case of a single channel system for 2WD cars.

3.2 Brake performance

Fig.4 shows the comparison of the braking distance on a low brake force coefficient road and directional stability on an asymmetric road. Improvement in the braking distance was expressed by comparison with the value of a 2WD car without an ASB system. The braking distance of a 4WD car was 5 per cent shorter than that of a 2WD car. A 4WD car equipped with a two channel ASB system showed 18 per cent shorter braking distance than a 2WD car and 4 per cent longer than a 2WD car equipped with a three channel ASB system. This small inferiority is considered to be caused not by the difference of control but by larger mass of inertia of 4WD drive line. Other test results of a 4WD car with centre differential unlocked equipped with a three channel ASB system showed equal braking distance to a 4WD car with a locked centre differential equipped with a two channel ASB system.

Stability on an asymmetric road was expressed by the angle of turn of a car from its original attitude during brake operation. A 4WD car with no ASB system equipped has shown the angle approximately twice as much as that of a 2WD car. This angle depends on suspension characteristics, especially kingpin offset at the ground. The tested car had plus offset. Other test results of a 4WD car with minus offset have shown 30 per cent larger angle of turn as compared with a 2WD car. Fig.6 shows the behaviour of a 4WD car with a two channel ASB system with front positioned sensors on an asymmetric road. Although a rear locked wheel on the lower coefficient side (wheel 3) was not controlled to reduce the fluid pressure, other rotating wheels forced wheel 3 to rotate through the drive line. In order to regain wheel speed, the brake force distribution must be designed as follows. Brake force of wheel 3 (BF3) is determined by the brake fluid pressure of wheel 2 on high coefficient road and ratio of front and rear brake forces. Driving force of wheel 3 is generated not only by inertia force of wheel 3 itself but also by of wheel 1 through the drive line. If the ratio is designed in such a way that the driving force for wheel 3 is larger than BF3, wheel 3 can regain speed. This control is similar to "select low control" of a three channel ASB system for 2WD cars.

3.3 Sensor position

Fig.7 shows the comparison of wheel speed sensitivity between front positioned sensors and the rear for the two channel ASB system. Front wheel rotational speed started to decrease a little earlier than rear since front brake torque was usually set larger than that of rear. Altough a delay of rear wheel lock was very small due to the high rigidity of a drive line, the two channel system with front positioned sensors showed better braking performance than the system with rear positioned sensors.

3.4 Comparision between single channel and two channel system

A 4WD car with a single channel ASB system showed less performance than that with a two channel ASB system because the

change of wheel rotational speed was calculated from the transfer shaft speed which averaged the change of each wheel speed as shown in Fig.8. Vehicle vibration of the single channel ASB system during ASB operation was larger than that of a two channel or a three channel system.

4 CONCLUSION

The behaviour of 4WD cars at braking was clarified through the experimental and mathmatical studies. A 4WD car has a higher limit of brake force than a 2WD car due to the constraint of the drive line. On the other hand, this constratint causes the two wheel lock on lower brake coefficient side and produces larger turning moment of the vehicle on an asymmetric road. Mathmatical simulation has shown good agreement with these test results.

The state of wheel lock ignoring transient state of a 4WD car is restricted mainly to all wheel lock or two wheel lock each in front and rear.

The two channel ASB system for a 4WD car with two sensors and two diagonally connected brake lines has shown almost similar improvement in braking distance and directional stability on an asymmetric road as compared with a three channel ASB system for a 2WD car. The two channel ASB system is mainly effective for full-time 4WD with centre differential locked or restricted by slip limiting devices. As to 2WD cars or selective 4WD cars, the two channel ASB system will reguire additional functions, such as yaw control to improve stability, additional wheel sensors, and so on.

REFERENCES

(1) Kageyama,K. Auto mobile engineering completion(JAPAN), Sankaido 135-152 ('85)
(2) Flegl,H.,Foldi,Th.,Witte,L. Handling characteristics of four-wheel drive vehicles. Dyn Veh Roads Tracs (USA) 165-178('84)
(3) Leiber,H. Antiskid System for Passenger Cars with a Digital Electric Control Unit. SAE790458
(4) Leiber,H.,Gzinczel,a. and Anlauf,J. Antiskid System(ASB) for Passenger Car. Bosch Technische Berichte,vol.7 No.2('80)
(5) Leiber,H.Gzinczel,A. Four Years of Experience with 4-wheel Anti skid Bake systems(ASB). SAE830481
(6) Hattig,P. Cost-Benefit Analysis of Simplified ASB. SAE50053

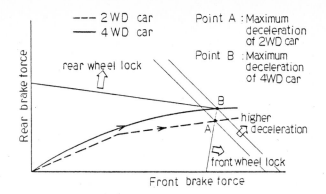

Fig 1   General characteristics of front and rear brake force
distribution for two-wheel drive and four-wheel drive cars

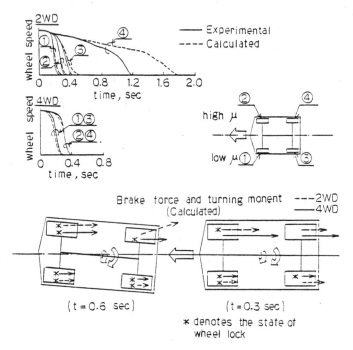

Fig 2

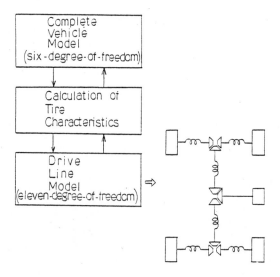

Fig 3   A mathematical simulation model similar to one developed by
Flegl *et al*

	diagram	Brake distance(*)	Angle of turn (**)
Two channel system 2 sensors 2 actuators independent control		0.82	0.08
Single channel system 1 sensor 2 actuators jointly control		0.87	0.14
Three channel system 4 sensors 4 actuators front indep rear jointly		0.78	0.05
2WD without ASB		1	1
4WD without ASB		0.95	2

(*) on a symmetric road
(**)on an asymmetric road

Fig 4   A schematic diagram of tested anti-skid brake systems

	State of wheel lock	Minimum number of sensors necessary to detect wheel lock
Four wheels lock		One sensor on the drive line
(a) Two wheels lock		Two sensors on front or rear wheels
(b) Diagonal two wheels lock		

▨ locked wheel

▢ unlocked wheel

Fig 5

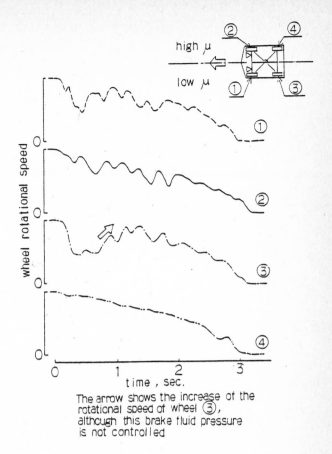

high μ
low μ

wheel rotational speed

① ② ③ ④

time , sec.

The arrow shows the increase of the rotational speed of wheel ③, although this brake fluid pressure is not controlled

Fig 6

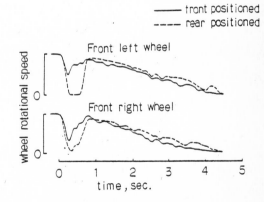

front positioned
---- rear positioned

Front left wheel

Front right wheel

wheel rotational speed

time , sec.

Fig 7   A comparison of wheel speed sensitivity between front positioned sensors and rear, for two-channel anti-skid brake system

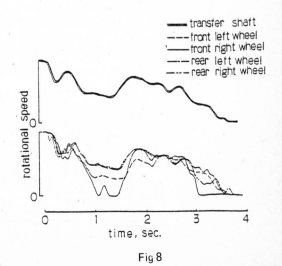

transfer shaft
---front left wheel
---front right wheel
---rear left wheel
---rear right wheel

rotational speed

time, sec.

Fig 8

C11/86

Design development and testing of the Sierra XRx4

J R W MANSFIELD, CEng, MIMechE
Ford Motor Company Limited, Research and Engineering Centre,
Laindon, Basildon, Essex

INTRODUCTION

It is not generally known that Ford had a
4 wheel drive vehicle with anti-skid
braking under serious consideration for
production in 1970. Four prototypes were
completed and were run and the project only
foundered because no suitable manufacturing
process could be established. The vehicle
selected was the 3.0 Capri and the system
was the Ferguson Formula with unequal
torque split, and a Dunlop Maxaret braking
system. At around the same time a fleet of
25 Zephyr and Zodiac estate cars were built
by Ferguson Research (as it was then) and
were used by several police forces for
evaluation – with great success.

Ford Advanced Vehicle Operations (AVO) were
in charge of the Capri project, and the
program was one of the first that that
organisation had planned. There were many
reasons for the project not proceeding;
the Maxaret braking system, for example,
was an adapted truck system and was rather
crude in operation, the brake pedal pumping
with considerable ferocity, as the servo
vacuum was being applied to alternate sides
of the diaphragm. The package in the Capri
was also extremely tight, particularly in
the area of the transmission tunnel, but
the main reason was that AVO did not have a
way at that time of getting to the body-
in-white during its assembly process, and
so all modifications to accept the 4 wheel
drive system had to be made on an already
completed vehicle. This was expensive and
inefficient, and would have had an adverse
effect on the corrosion resistance and the
assembly quality of the vehicle.

The dynamic operation of the vehicles was
excellent; the vastly superior traction
being a great improvement over the normal
3.0 litre Capri which was noted for its
tail happiness, with 1970 tyre technology
and lots of low down torque from the Essex
engine, all in a light car. The principle
was proved by the dominance of the 4 wheel
drive Capri Rallycross cars built by
Boreham Competitions and successfully
campaigned by Roger and Stan Clark and Rod
Chapman (see fig.1).

By 1982 therefore, when it was proposed
that Ford should display a four wheel drive
Sierra at the Frankfurt show for the launch
of the Sierra, there was a lot of company

knowledge about the Ferguson formula four
wheel drive system in particular, and it
was hardly surprising that this company was
chosen to build the show car. The aim was
to have a driveable car for press appraisal
but to show standards as a technical flag
waving exercise. It was to be built as a
2.3 litre Ghia manual 5-door (the XR4i was
not in production at this time) and was
constructed by F.F. Developments (as they
now were) with a short 6 months design,
development and build time.

F.F. Developments produced the vehicle on
time, but during that 6 months span the
product planners had been active. It
became apparent that the fashion for
4 wheel drive, started in 1980 by Audi had
been gathering pace. Although the Audi
sales of 4WD were nothing spectactular (95
in 1981 and 154 in 1982 in Britain, with
less than 3500 total in Europe up to the
end of 1982) the Subaru had been quietly
making significant inroads to the market
place, particularly in Austria and
Switzerland. In 1982, for example, they
built more than 18,000 vehicles (1691 in
Britain) showing that the practical
advantages of 4 wheel drive were being
appreciated by customers, particularly in
European territories which had a
significantly long winter spell.

The Sierra concept car suddenly therefore
had more significance than just a technical
show piece – it became the leading design
for a full Sierra 4 wheel drive program
that was looking financially viable as well
as being a technological exercise. For
this reason it was 'pulled' from the 1982
Frankfurt show and 3 further concept cars
were commissioned from F.F. Developments.

CONCEPT CARS
By late '82 the project for designing and
developing a 4 wheel drive Sierra for
production was under way and the task was
entrusted to my company's relatively new
Special Vehicle Engineering (SVE) department. This department was formed in 1980
for many of the same reasons that AVO was
formed in 1970. These were: the need for
us to be able to respond quickly to new
marketing trends (and 4 wheel drive for
passenger cars was one of these); to
engineer small volume production cars
(defined as being around 5,000-10,000
vehicles per year); and to provide Ford of

Europe with good image vehicles such as two of the previous SVE programs, the Capri 2.8 injection and the Fiesta XR2 (see fig.2).

Many of the problems of AVO had been avoided by positioning SVE as an integral part of the Product Development group and by ensuring that SVE vehicles could be built down the same production lines as all other volume products. AVO had had its own production line for 25-30 cars per day (see fig.3) separated from all other Ford manufacturing facilities and the 1974 fuel crisis had shown that the organisation was not flexible enough to weather a production down-turn.

The concept for the vehicles was confirmed as a Ferguson Formula high performance, high specification car at the top end of the Sierra range using viscous couplings to control wheel slip and pioneering anti-skid braking on four wheel drive vehicles by using the Teves ABS system already planned to be introduced on the new Granada range at about the same time as the Sierra 4x4 would be going into production. A strong desire that there should be no extra controls for the driver to operate (and perhaps mis-use) also led to the choice of the FF system.

The first task was to meet with Teves and to establish jointly if we believed the ABS system could work with 4 wheel drive. The problem was the unknown amount of inter-reaction provided between the front and rear axles, and across the rear axle by the viscous couplings. Teves considered that they could tailor their system, which sensed the rotational frequency of all four wheels, to cater for all conditions but they needed a vehicle for assessment under low μ conditions as soon as possible. Two of the four concept cars were directed towards this investigation as soon as they were completed (August 1982 and February 1983).

Teves winter test location in Northern Sweden was then the scene for an extensive investigation on different ratings of viscous coupling to establish the point above which the viscous coupling would have an adverse effect on the ABS. Concurrently SVE were establishing the lowest level of interaction that would give all the advantages of locking differentials, and a suitable compromise was found that met all these parameters.

Two further concept cars were completed by F.F. Developments, and one was immediately put on to the Ford start-stop test to assess the overall durability of the system. This test consists of a cycle of maximum acceleration torques being applied to a vehicle loaded to gross vehicle weight together with torque reversals at the maximum torque revs, through all the gears, repeated for 2,400 cycles. As the follow-on program for the Granada Scorpio 4x4 had also been considered at this stage, the loading for this test was that of the top of the range Scorpio.

DESIGN PROCESS

The concept cars were proving out the principle of the program - SVE's task was to redesign all the parts for volume production. Packaging was to be suitable for volume production; servicing of the components was to be nothing out of the ordinary; assembly was to be adequate for a production line running at the rate of 45 vehicles/hour; and durability was to be at the same standard as any other production vehicle. The disposition of all the components in the transfer case was changed to save space (over 100mm was removed from the overall transmission length partly by relocating the speedo drive gear from the gearbox mainshaft to the front axle); intrusion into the passenger compartment was greatly reduced by optimising the design; removal of the front axle from the side of the sump needed to be made possible for servicing without taking the engine out; and all the engine add-on components for the front axle needed to be redesigned to suit assembly and hot test in the Cologne engine plant without disrupting the engine line (see fig.4).

This redesign process resulted in the engine being moved a small amount in the engine bay, some 4mm to the left of the vehicle, and some 4mm upwards at the front. Items which gave particular package problems were the starter motor, the clutch housing and operating mechanism, the rear engine mounting and the steering shaft for the rack and pinion and perhaps most of all the engine front cross member.

This latter unit is a fabricated steel component in the base car, with the functions of providing front engine mounting positions, pivot points for the inner ends of the track control arms for the front suspension, and for the steering rack. Adding to these requirements the necessary clearance for all the entire front axle and driveshaft components, the fabricated steel cross member became just too complex. An aluminium casting in heat-treated LM24 solved this problem, and incidentally sliced $1/2 million off our tooling bill with a weight saving of over 3Kg, although the piece price was increased.

DEVELOPMENT

A prototype program was established to enable this design to be proved out prior to production. For this program ten vehicles were needed, and a build process started which resulted in the first prototype being available by July 1983 and the last one was completed by July 1984. Vehicles were used for further start/stop testing; for 40,000 miles General Durability; for High Speed testing; for homologation actions; for ride and handling development; for brake testing; for cold climate appraisal; for crash test; for Noise Vibration and Harshness work and for all the other development and testing tasks that are required to be done. No significant failures were recorded during this development program, although some interesting points arose. For example,

42

© IMechE 1986 C11/86

when a vehicle was damaged on a front corner, a potential field problem was demonstrated; with one front wheel trapped by damaged sheet metal, a suspended tow caused the other front wheel to rotate at twice towing speed which looked quite bizarre. Service instructions had to be given that suspended tows from either front or rear wheels could not be conducted because the centre LSD would operate, and an overheating would gradually bring the rotating wheels to rest. (Removal of the propshaft is necessary under these conditions.)

Cold climate testing with snow chains showed up another peculiarity:
although a 4 wheel drive vehicle does not need snow chains under any but the most extreme conditions (a 4 wheel drive vehicle on summer tyres is much more than the equal of a 2 wheel drive vehicle with snow chains; and a 4 wheel drive vehicle with winter tyres is virtually unstoppable), legal requirements dictate that it must be possible to fit snow chains. Assessment of the snow chain operation in Finland indicated that the vehicle was difficult to drive with chains fitted to the rear wheels only - only when chains were fitted to the front wheels did the vehicle become stable. Therefore do not assume that the driver has made a mistake next time you see a Sierra with snow chains on the front wheels only.

Ride and handling development was conducted to give sporting vehicle characteristics with fairly neutral handling, good turn in and a level ride, exploiting to the full the 4 wheel drive characteristics. Thus stiffer roll bars were specified with firmer damping and the sharper handling was largely achieved by fitting plastic ball joints to the front inner track control arms instead of the conventional rubber bushes. Additionally variable ratio steering gear was adopted which gives an effective 3.28 turns lock to lock ratio in the straight ahead position and a 2.75 on lock (power steering is standard).

Good results of 56mm static steering wheel intrusion were achieved in the 30 mph barrier crash test. In this case the increased strength of the cast cross member held the front end of the car together particularly well in the impact.

Noise Vibration and Harshness development was largely centred around the structural stiffness of the engine/transmission unit and the positioning and effectiveness of the rear engine mount. Considerable lateral vibrations were transmitted to the floor pan through the rear mount at an engine speed of 2800 rpm. Increased rigidity of the floor pan in this area gave a good improvement so a production fix was established to cover the early production cars. "Betabrace" was applied to the tunnel in the rear mounting area at the body-in-white stage, and was effectively cured by subsequent passage through the paint ovens. This rather temporary but effective solution was only needed for a small number of early vehicles. Vehicles from September 1984 had a modified floor pan which was much stiffer laterally and thus the vibration was no longer a concern.

Almost inevitably prototype Sierra 4x4s exhibited a variety of transmission and driveline noises. A major concern was what was first considered to be a front axle whine coupled with a transfer box ringing. This phenomena manifested itself at 2 or 3 peaks, dependent upon vehicle, at 15.5:31 and 46,5 times the engine speed in direct drive (4th gear). Since the chain wheels have 31 teeth they were suspected as the source or at least as transmitters. The solution was found by introducing a controlled "inaccuracy" in the circular tooth pitch of one of the chain wheels. This had the effect of breaking up the generated frequencies.

Despite the fact that the viscous coupling design had been around for some 18 years it was first used in significant quantities on the Escort RS Turbo, which program was very shortly followed by the Sierra 4x4 using two of them. Because it was new to my company (and to the motor industry in general) there was no established manufacturing source and no background experience to indicate the magnitude and duration of any slip speeds or torque transmissions the units would be called upon to bear. Therefore we had to establish some tests which worked the units to temperatures and internal pressures that would be unlikely or even impossible to be achieved in service. We drove the vehicles for many miles with either the front or the rear drive shafts disconnected so that the whole engine torque is being handled by the centre viscous coupling (it is difficult to detect any difference in driving character-istics under these conditions). We towed an XR4i with an XR4x4 with its front driveshaft removed, and periodically applied the brakes on the towed vehicle - this way we were able to establish the relationship between differential speeds across the couplings, temperature build up and torque transmitted.

A peculiarity of the viscous coupling design is the possibility of making the unit "hump" - that is when transmitting a significant amount of torque over a period of time, the temperature rise can at a predetermined point cause the unit to become much stiffer by a factor of 4 or 5 times (see fig.5). This is a function of viscosity, temperature of operation and percentage of fluid fill inside the sealed unit. Development units were humped by driving up inclines and transmitting torque through a stalled unit until failure (the failure mode is destruction of the seals allowing the silicon fluid to escape). Changes introduced on the units due to this development testing included the intro-duction of a nitrided finish on the plates as the original plates were found to be too soft, and introduction of spiral grooves on the bearing surfaces to improve lubrication.

Apart from the deliberate failures discussed above the units have proved to be remarkably trouble free in operation. This gives us confidence that they are working well within their capacity, and as our knowledge increases such devices will become smaller and more compact and thus cheaper for future programs.

MANUFACTURE

The vehicle Job 1 was on April 24, 1985 following a preproduction build of 26 cars in March. The car was announced at the Geneva Motor Show and five vehicles were available for Press driving purposes (see fig.6). The reception was very good with the plus features of superb traction being well displayed with a drive up the Col de Turini. The ABS was introduced separately with the 1986MY vehicle five months later in September 1985. Considerations when putting this 4 wheel drive vehicle into a plant normally associated with 2 wheel drive included the requirement to turn one front wheel relative to the other (without turning the rear wheels) through 180 deg. on the track setting equipment (resolved by rotating one wheel backwards and the other wheel forwards); the adverse effect of the moving tracks on the floors which progress the vehicles through the plant (no concern - the viscous coupling speed differential is so low that there is no significant torque transfer) and a rememberance that one cannot put one end of the car on a chassis dyno without allowing the other wheels to rotate also.

Concerns apparent in the launch phase were small, and related almost entirely to the normal issues with any vehicle such as fit and finish and availability of all the correct parts.

CONCLUSIONS

The concept of 4 wheel drive has certainly been well launched within Ford. So far the vehicle has been trouble free in service and the production volumes have greatly exceeded the planning volume for the program. The concept has been well received by the press and public throughout Europe, and I should like to thank the Directors of Ford Motor Company for permission to publish this paper.

Fig 1   Four-wheel drive rallycross Capri three-litre under test

Fig 2   Ford Special Vehicle Engineering Department (SVE) with some of their products

44

Fig 3   Ford advanced vehicle operations production line in 1970

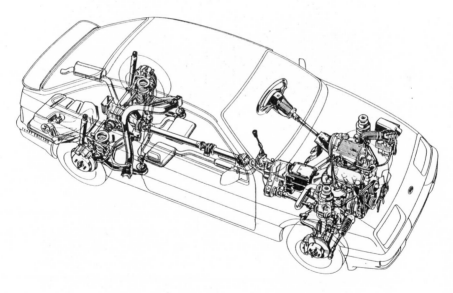

Fig 4   General cutaway of Sierra XR4 x 4

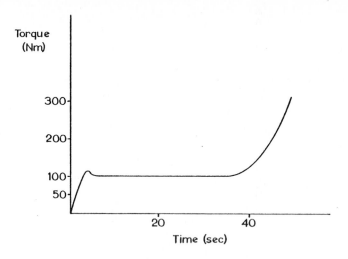

Fig 5   Diagram showing the hump characteristics of the viscous coupling

Fig 6   Sierra XR4 x 4 in the Swiss Alps

Four-wheel drive Grand Prix cars

J MILES
London

A review of the events leading up to the adoption of four wheel drive by some teams for the 1969 Grand Prix season, and a discussion of the handling behaviour (and development) of these and other four wheel drive racing cars as seen through the eyes of the drivers and designers concerned.

It is probably fair to say that the traction advantages of four wheel drive were first seen on steam locomotives. Where automobiles are concerned, it all started with the Spyker, conceived in 1902 by Joseph Laviolette. Several four wheel drive hill climb specials followed. There was the 1931 T53 Bugatti. Harry Armenius Miller, visionary that he was, had a four wheel drive Indianapolis car running in 1932 - others followed, though none were very successful. After the war there was the ill-fated Porsche designed Cisitalia Grand Prix car, then not much until the brilliant Harry Ferguson marshalled his tiny company's resources and produced the 1.5 litre Climax engined P99 in which Stirling Moss won a streaming wet Oulton Park Gold Cup in 1961. In the light of subsequent events, we can only suggest why the P99 was demonstrably superior in the wet at Oulton Park and Aintree, because other 4 x 4 GP cars did not enjoy the same success. Jack Fairman took the car to Indianapolis for tests, where it impressed the likes of Andy Granatelli with its speed through the turns. The Granatelli financed supercharged Novi V8 Ferguson Indianapolis cars followed, and it was bits and pieces of these that were actually incorporated into the STP Paxton turbine car that would have easily won the 1967 race but for a transmission bearing failure seven miles from the finish.

Lotus' Colin Chapman and Andy Granatelli clearly felt four wheel drive was the way to go even though the STP Paxton car's performance had prompted the governing body USAC to reduce the turbine inlet annulus from 23.999 sq in to 15.999 sq in, which would limit outputs to about 500 bhp. Chapman was right. After a disasterous test session when Mike Spence was killed, it was Joe Leonard and Graham Hill who occupied the first two places on the grid for the 1968 race. Hill crashed, but Leonard and Pollard could have won but for the failure of "fail safe" fuel pump shafts fitted at the insistence of Pratt and Whitney engineers. Later came the Bignotti Lolas which were also quick with a Hewland developed four wheel drive system.

Picture the scene back in Europe. In 1968 Grand Prix cars were sprouting massive suspension attached wings (Fig. 1) which were beginning to break up as designers applied more and more downforce. At the Spanish Grand Prix both Jochen Rindt and Graham Hill had potentially fatal accidents on the streets of Barcelona (Fig. 2). Without thought the CSI reacted by banning wings altogether, then compromised by permitting far smaller body mounted aerodynamic devices.

Meanwhile Chapman and Duckworth were already working on their four wheel drive GP cars. Suddenly those teams with four wheel drive programmes seemed to hold all the aces, and for Lotus there was the 56B Formula One turbine car to come.

The design philosophy in the 4 x 4 GP car was to get as close as feasible to a 50/50 weight distribution.

By definition most of the 4 x 4 contenders had a longer wheelbase than their RWD counterparts. They also had heavy drive componentry added up front, specifically the forward drive casing, gears, differential, plus driveshafts, and the encased shaft running forward from the torque split which was usually of Ferguson epicyclic design, all of which added around 130 lbs in weight (Fig. 3). They all had their Cosworth DFV's turned through 180 deg, and mated to a specially developed clutch housing and foreshortened Hewland gearbox, before the drive was stepped sideways by gears to the torque split unit on the left hand side of the driver. Even without the addition of drive to the front wheels, none of these extra components contributed to handling response.

What four wheel drive enthusiasts could not have anticipated was the huge improvement in tyres that occured over the next season, or how much downforce could be achieved even with the much smaller body mounted aerodynamic devices that replaced the suspension mounted wings. As it turned out RWD Grand Prix cars simply did not have the expected traction problems. On the other hand four wheel drive GP cars of the 1969 season did suffer from several undesirable handling traits. Before detailing these, it is important to explain the function of the driver in a conventional rear wheel drive racing car.

Regardless of the amount of power or grip available, the driver depends on maneouvrability, ie. response. The driver also needs a car that is in balance because a car that is neither understeering nor oversteering significantly is making best use of the tyre grip available at each end. It is well understood that racing cars (and road cars for that matter) depend for their balance on the careful tuning of springs, dampers, anti roll bars and aerodynamic downforce when applicable, but even then a driver is only likely to be able to tune a car to perfection for corners in a certain speed envelope. Ultimately he depends on his ability to modify the balance of the car with reflex movements of the steering and throttle. He is constantly and instantaneously making tiny adjustments in balance as the car is sliding. In most circumstances this ability to instantaneously maintain control over both ends of the car is also considered vital as track conditions change, or the adhesion limit is overstepped, or simply to accommodate different driving styles. Our experience showed that by "coupling" the front and rear, the driver lost this flexibility of control.
Talk to the driver of any four wheel drive racing car, Stirling Moss included, and they will describe a loss in controllability; a loss in the ability to balance the car with steering and throttle.

Lack of straight line speed was often cited as a reason for the slow lap times achieved by most FWD GP cars. My experience was that they were two or three mph slower on the straights, but the principle reason for disappointment was the lack of manoeuvrability, reduced controllability, and understeer (Fig. 4). The rally car case is a special one where the drivers use left foot braking and other techniques to overcome the lack of conventional controllability. As things stand in motor racing there is more grip available so such techniques are not feasible since one cannot afford any waste of engine power. The reactions and sensitivity necessary would also be beyond even the best driver's capabilities, since the speeds involved are so high.

The key point is that whereas the balance of a RWD racing car is ultimately at the discretion of the driver, who has control of both ends of the car, the balance of a 4WD racing car is essentially "in the car." In testing the Lotus 63, this was made all too clear. Regardless of its deficiencies, all drivers achieved the same lap times quite easily, whereas it took me two or three times the number of laps to get within half a second of Jochen Rindt if we were testing a RWD Lotus 72. This was because he had a finer feeling of balance and the better car control that goes with it. He could fully exploit the 72, whereas Lotus 63 balance was inbuilt, leaving its limits well defined and barely unalterable. Most of the season, torque splits were in the 40/60, 30/70 range. With this kind of torque balance it was a directionally stable car - too stable in fact. Except at very low speeds, understeer was always the limitation. If one turned into bends on a trailing throttle, or under braking (a normal RWD technique) the car would start swinging rather pendulously into oversteer, and there was no point of maintainable balance between these two extremes. Steering loads were also high. Set up sliding on its ideal line there were no controllability problems, but if you went into a corner a little too fast or on slightly the wrong line, one could only lift off the throttle and wait for the attitude to change before starting all over again. The car did not respond to small movements of steering and throttle, which could have re-balanced a RWD car in mid corner according to the driver's wishes.

In the quest for better balance (less understeer) the amount of torque to the front wheels was progressively reduced as the season wore on. It is now clear that this attempt to make a four wheel drive racer with close to 50/50 weight distribution behave more like a rear wheel drive car was not the right way to go. I now feel that improvements in lap times were due more to chassis and aerodynamic development than changes in the torque split. For example, we started the season qualifying around 4½ secs behind pole position man. The best practice performance was at Mosport where the 63 (with a 30/70 torque split) qualified 2.6 sec behind Ickx's pole position Brabham. Earlier in the year Mario Andretti had crashed a 63 at the Nurburgring after qualifying second to last. At the Oulton Park Gold Cup Jochen Rindt practiced 3 sec slower than pole position and managed a distant second (its best race finish), 82 secs behind in a poorly supported 40 lap race. Otherwise it was gearbox, fuel pump problems, or crashes that sidelined the car. By this time MacLaren had long since given up any idea of pursuing the concept. Tyrell were soldiering on with their out of date (and torsionally unrigid) spaceframe MS84 with very little more success than Lotus, while the Cosworth never got beyond the testing stage (Fig. 5). Those who persisted could not wait for it to rain. Colin Chapman and Mario Andretti got their wish during practice for the US Grand Prix at Watkins Glen. Mario did 1m 19.6 sec against Jack Brabham's 1m 13.84 sec. In the dry he returned 1m 6.52 sec compared with Rindt's 1m 3.62 sec. Mario was fifth from slowest on both occasions!

Not long after I had the opportunity to drive a 63 at Snetterton in the wet, and understood why Mario hadn't shone at Watkins Glen. By this time the car was running a 12.5/87.5 torque split, making the whole concept of four wheel drive utterly pointless. Such a torque balance did reduce the understeer especially in slow corners where the grip of the tyres could be overcome, but the car was still terribly ungainly; the rear sliding ponderously outwards, while the driver applied liberal quantities of opposite lock with the steering heavying up uncomfortably. In the same situation the RWD racers would turn in far quicker, get the power on, and be nicely balanced powering neatly out of the same hairpin with little if any wheelspin. They had the response, the control, and no lack of grip, even at speed where the aerodynamic aids were least effective. In the wet, one only had to begin to feed in the DFV's considerable torque

to set the rear wheels spinning, driving the car into a pendulous slide. In the wet there was far more power than traction and even less control. The "torque" balance totally dominated, and I vividly recall spinning as soon as any decent throttle opening was applied and there was nothing whatever I could do about it.

In retrospect, it was silly not to have developed a limited slip device for the centre differential, as this might have moderated the sudden rear wheelspin present in poor conditions.

Other comments supplied for this paper on the subject of four wheel drive competition car handling make interesting reading.

Keith Duckworth

"Once wings had arrived, any benefit of four wheel drive had vanished. I refused to go below 30 percent to the front wheels on the grounds, that if you could not make it work with that, it was no good because you could not justify the weight, complication, and reduced response. With that much torque going through the front wheels you always have the potential for front wheelspin (although modern limited slip devices might reduce the problem, which obviously increase as the power to weight ratio goes up). We had a true 50/50 weight distribution, the same geometries, same wheels and tyres, to try and make a balanced car. That put us in the position of having to use limited slip diffs front and rear. We couldn't even get round the normally flat out Abbey curve at Silverstone without lifting off because the diffs were effectively locked and the car wanted to go straight on. Throughout the acceleration curve (just about all the time on the track) the front wheels are likely to be on the point of slipping. Wide tyres dictated that you couldn't have centre point steering, so the driver was fighting constantly varying steering forces. The cars gradually went down to 20/80 and even more rear biased torque splits (2½ wheel drive!) which was pointless."

Maurice Phillippe (Chief Designer at Lotus 1965 - 1971 and presently Chief Designer at Tyrrell).

"I arrived in G.P. car design at the time the formula was changing from 1.5 litre unsupercharged to 3.0 litre unsupercharged engine capacity and the expression "Return to Power" was the bye-word. This implied that traction was going to be a problem. At the time at Lotus, we were looking at the H-16 B.R.M. engine, which had an access hole through the block for a 4WD driveshaft. Knowing Colin would require my opinion about 4WD, I prepared some notes, coming out in favour of 2WD on the basis that under acceleration the 2WD had nearly all its weight, due to weight transfer, on the rear wheels anyway, so traction was not going to manifest itself as a problem. I also noted the "balance response" possible by the driver with 2WD would be lost with 4WD. Accordingly, there were no 4WD cars at Lotus until the advent of the turbine car for Indianapolis.

An Indy 4WD car with a turbine engine was a totally different matter. First, we had evidence of the STP car from the previous year as a guide on the high speed handling and then there were the turbine engine characteristics. This made driving the long turns at Indy a relatively smooth affair, as the turbine was never allowed to idle at less than 80% gas generator speed, and the brakes were used to control speed and initial acceleration against the idle drive of the engine. All this with a 40:60 torque split amounted to a reasonable performance with 550 h.p. available at 110% gas generator speed.

When Cosworth threatened to build a 4WD G.P. car several teams followed suit (despite misgivings). If Keith was going to do it, then it had to be the way to go! The Cosworth car had the shortest track life of any G.P. car, 4WD or not! Meanwhile, Lotus amongst others soldiered on to a final conclusion.

Now we can't use 4WD any way due to legislation. However, you should note that we are now handling up to three times the power available during the 3 litre unsupercharged formula, and two wheels seem to cope reasonably well despite limitations on tyre size.

The driver is still a useful commodity for sorting out the transient balance situation. Allowing for such goodies as viscous diffs and black box magic, the prospect for 4WD G.P. cars would not be very high in my opinion, even were it allowed to be used. Weight and the need for a very comprehensive "drive by wire" system would obviate any marginal gain in performance of a car on a smooth surface."

Ken Tyrrell

"Our experience with the MS84 was similar to that of Lotus. In an unusually dry year, it finally rained for the practice at Watkins Glen and here was the test we had waited for. Our disappointment in discovering that the 2 wheel drive car was quicker than the 4 wheel drive version was tempered by the relief of not having to design and race 4WD versions the following year."

Rudi Ulenhaut (Mercedes G.P. Team Engineer/Driver).

"We were conducting experiments - if the opposition had been there we would have responded with 4 wheel drive."

Tony Rudd

"The BRM T67 was 12 mph slower on the straight at Snetterton in the hands of Richie Ginther and no faster through the corners, so we lost interest, particularly as we were neck and neck with Lotus and a revived Ferrari for the world championship and we could no longer spare something like 25% of the effort in men and resources to work on the car.

It is all best summed up in a conversation I had with Bruce MacLaren where I said we could have gone slow easier and cheaper with a hundredweight bag of sand, an immersion heater in the oil tank, and a throttle stop limiting us to 90% of the power, or a police flasher unit on the roof. Richie summed it up by saying he could never tell what its limits were going to be until he was in the bushes."

Mike Pilbeam (Designer at Lotus and currently running his own race car design company).

"On a pre-set line a four wheel drive racing car was reasonable, but there was nothing a driver could do to modify its behaviour for changing radius corners. There was a loss of response due to the additional weight up front and the front wheel drive torque. Perhaps it's time to think again about four wheel drive for hill climb cars. This certainly would be if tyre and aerodynamic restrictions were imposed."

Bill Milliken (well known to most of you as a highly analytical engineer and talented driver) drove Archie Butterworth's 4 x 4 special 'Butterball' and the Four Wheel Drive Auto Company's 'FWD Special', a four wheel drive Miller, the latter into 6th place at the

19 mile long Pike's Peak hill climb in 1949 (Fig. 6). The surface is loose gravel and dirt. He ran the car with the central differential unlocked and locked, and found that on loose surfaces a fixed transmission system was essential in preventing random wheelslip.

"Providing all four wheels were actually being driven more or less equally its performance was excellent, but before the centre differential was locked, any misjudgement in the application of power usually resulted in one or both rear wheels losing traction, randomly leading to an uncontrollable spin. Even when the car could be controlled, torque would go increasingly to the wheels that had already broken traction accentuating the initial breakaway as the torque was relieved on the wheels where the traction remained intact. The car was similarly unstable under braking with the rear wheels locking randomly. Locking the centre differential transformed the car, enabling it to traverse the course at substantially higher speed with no sign of instability. If a bend was taken at excessive speed, the car would merely drift sideways without a change in heading, the amount of drift being readily controllable by the amount of power applied."

Stirling Moss (Ferguson P99) also liked four wheel drive.

"Once you had started a manoeuvre you were far more committed with the Ferguson (with a rear wheel drive car you can modify the line a bit with steering and throttle). You needed to completely alter one's driving style. You needed tremendous precision, but its roadholding in the wet was stupendous. It was so good, I could drive round the outside of most Grand Prix cars (Fig. 7) - I passed Phil Hill's Dino Ferrari on the outside at Aintree. The brakes were stunning. The most difficult thing was being fast enough to get off the brakes back on to the throttle. You could go in so 'deep' it was incredible. Apart from its speed at Aintree and winning the Gold Cup (and subsequently winning the RAC Hill Climb Championship), I think its potential was hidden by lack of consistant success."

Jochen Rindt (Lotus 63) was quite succinct.

"You can't 'race' the car."

Tony Rolt (FF Developments)

"Four wheel drive was dogged by bad luck and lack of development, but look at the STP Paxton, Lotus 56, and P99. In the 1969 season it was hard to get the tyre people to bother much when their efforts were so well rewarded in the RWD cars. The MS84 Matra was a spaceframe so torsionally unrigid that anti roll car adjustments had very little effect. When Johnny Servos Gavin drove it in the final GP of the season at Mexico we disconnected the drive to the front wheels and he couldn't tell any difference in the handling! It was that sort of car. Tyres and aerodynamic developments ruined the potential for four wheel drive on the circuit - but I agree that the addition of drive to the front wheels robs the car of cornering force normally used to "balance" a rear wheel drive racing car. The driver cannot materially affect the balance which is inbuilt."

Rene Dreyfus (T53 Bugatti)

"It did have some advantages - stopping and starting on wet roads - but the car was impossible to drift. Whatever direction you aimed it, that was the direction it went. Accuracy and a tendency not to hesitate were called for. I could handle that. The strength of Hercules was also called for. That I couldn't." (Fig 8).

Mauri Rose (FWD Miller at Indianapolis)

"You can't throw this vehicle around - there is no independent control of the rear end. I just steered it round."

Mario Andretti (Lotus 56 Turbine at Indianapolis)

"Four wheel drive has stability advantages at Indianapolis - I was quickest through the turns in the 56. Its stability was great, but you needed a more committed driving style."

Mario Andretti (Lotus 63 Grand Prix car)

"The problem was that by the time it came along there was no traction problem anyway. There were frictional losses. The car wouldn't change direction, and it was too heavy."

Parnelli Jones raced a Lotus 56 at Riverside road circuit.

For Riverside he ran torque splits in the 30/70 or even 20/80 range (Lotus ran 45/55 at Indy) and liked the car's balance - though crashed the car.

Bobby Unser (V8 Novi Ferguson)

Having tried all the closer to equal options, he used a 30/70 torque split at Indianapolis. Although he experienced marked trailing throttle oversteer, it was declared "not a problem."

Derek Bell (Mclaren M9A 1969 British Grand Prix)

"The problem was that you could not control the car. It would do nothing but understeer unless I resorted to vicious driving techniques to upset the rear end and then it was slower still."

Bruce Mclaren (Mclaren M9A)

"Driving the M9A was like trying to sign your name with somebody jogging your elbow!"

Jackie Stewart

"The heavy steering wasn't a problem. The biggest problem was the front end understeering under power and not being able to get rid of the understeer either by deceleration or trailing throttle going into a corner and reapplying power. You would get the car going into a 'half neutral position', apply the power, and you had to be a real artist to be able to catch it at the right moment to have what would really amount to having a four wheel drift. It only happened once every six corners. You were doing a balancing act to accommodate the inadequacies of the front end not to take control. Altering steering and throttle didn't have the same effect in getting more grip at the front end, or breaking away the rear as it would in a rear wheel drive car. That was the frustration of it. In a course like Silverstone for example where you were going through long radius corners it was worse because you had to live with this feeling for a longer period, whereas if it were a stop and go type of situation it might have been more bearable.

The Matra had similar characteristics in the wet as in the dry but worse, because again the amount of space available is less because the period of recovery is longer. Thinking back I might have been a little more tentative going into a corner because I learned that as soon as you applied the power I had immediate "washout". Turning in wasn't a problem until you started going off the trailing throttle to get into a neutral throttle and then on to full throttle. As soon as you went off a trailing throttle back on to the power the car's 'head' started to go towards the front end."

While other teams gave up in disgust Colin Chapman persisted. He wanted a "second string" car that could at least guarantee a finish - hence the Lotus 56B. The Pratt and Whitney PT6 turbine was a trusty unit in helicopters and the Indianapolis breakdowns had only been silly failures. United Aircraft co-operated by providing technical back up and a PT6 with two stages of the three stage axial gasifier removed to improve response. Starting a race with 75 gallons of JP4 fuel aboard the 56B ran heavy compared with a piston engined car. It was virtually an Indianapolis car with Formula One wings, the drive being taken straight from the turbine output shaft to the epicyclic torque splitter via a Morse chain.

There was no gearbox of course, and just two giant size pedals either side of the steering column. Like any turbine it only started producing real power between 80 and 100 percent of its gasifier's output. Throttle lag was between 2 and 3 seconds which was obviously a problem on European circuits, whereas at Indianapolis speeds were so high there was much less of a response problem. By virtue of the speeds involved, steer angles were tiny, and there was far less excess torque available. Even with the 45/55 torque split used, understeer did not seem to be a problem, whereas the gain in stability at the very high speeds involved was considerable.

The Formula One 56B had huge ventilated discs and double thickness pads. Even so, with 70 bhp going through the transmission even with right foot off the throttle, brake pad wear was phenomenal. Braking had to be initiated earlier than in RWD car, then one had to start building up the power against the brakes on the entry to the corner. Before the apex, both feet were planted firmly on both pedals, balancing huge contradicting forces. Your right foot was hard down on the throttle and to accelerate you eased back progressively on the brakes. Clearly, the faster one lapped the more the brakes came into play.

It was a car that required even more planning and commitment than the 63 to drive at the limit. It was also wonderfully quiet; there was no vibration. The roar of the exhaust seemed to get left behind the faster the car went. Over bumps you could hear the pads rattling in the calipers, the clattering of the solid jointed suspension, and there was usually some tyre squeal in the dry. I left Lotus after Jochen Rindt was killed in practice for the 1970 Italian Grand Prix, so never got to race the turbine F1 car. In the dry it was only a low to mid field runner with Fittipaldi, Wisell, or Walker. By contrast it showed real promise in the wet. Fittipaldi qualified in the middle of the front row at Brands Hatch (1971 Race of the Champions) which was hardly suited to the car or driving techniques involved.

At the beginning of the 1971 Dutch Grand Prix the weather changed for the worse, and the relatively inexperienced Dave Walker went from 22nd place on the grid to 10th in five laps before crashing. For a moment four wheel drive looked good just as it had been for Moss a decade before. Now it is banned in both formulae, so we can only make some suggestions as to why the turbine worked reasonably well in the wet (when four wheel drive was supposed to come into its own) and the 63 didn't, and why the Ferguson P99 went so well.

Before he died, I spoke to Colin Chapman on the subject. He felt that the wet weather behaviour of the turbine cars was due to their power characteristics. There were none of the sudden on/off torque reversals present in a piston engined car. He also felt that four wheel drive worked best in situations of low driving torque, ie. at high speeds when the stability gain was really worth something, or in the wet when the smooth turbine power curve was a distinct advantage.

In fact there may have been more to it. We shall never know how much of the turbines wet weather performance was due to tyres (the 15 in dia wheel and tyres would have given a longer contact patch), but I have felt the steadying influence and reduction in body movement left foot braking can have, a technique drivers of the 56B had to adopt. Left foot braking appears to inhibit the unpleasant attitude changes due to weight transfer. It is also better understood that a tyre may generate more cornering force while simultaneously subject to moderate braking. The transition to an accelerating mode in a turbine would be very smooth with left foot braking. It has also been suggested that the almost continuous braking action could also have been acting like a very effective wheelspin limiting device (some manufacturers are now using the brakes to limit wheelspin).

Disregarding Indianapolis experience, the Ferguson P99 stands out (as Stirling Moss' experiences testify) as the only really successful four wheel drive Grand Prix car, in the dry when four wheel drive was not expected to excel. On the first day of practice for the British GP at Aintree it was dry and Moss recorded 2m 00.6 sec.
Fastest man, Phil Hill, (Ferrari) who returned 1m 58.6 sec. Practice the following day was damp, and Moss was fastest with 2m 01.6 sec (astonishingly close to his dry weather lap time), no less than 4 sec faster than Salvadori (Cooper). Next up was Von Trips' Ferrari with 2m .06.0 sec. The race was wet and when Moss took over from Jack Fairman, he started lapping 2 sec faster than the leaders, returning a 2m 00.8 sec lap before the car was disqualified for an earlier push start.

At the Gold Cup, Moss put the Ferguson in the middle of the front row with 1m 44.8 sec, 0.2 sec behind pole position man Brabham in a Cooper. The race was mostly damp and Moss won by 45 sec. Its 1½ litre Coventry Climax engine would have been producing around 150 bhp so even with a dry weight of 1,090 lbs, its power to weight ratio could not compare with later 3 litre GP cars which had 430 bhp and weighed around 1,200 lbs dry. This fact coupled with a lack of downforce and much narrower tyres clearly prevented some of the problems experienced in later four wheel drive GP cars. The Ferguson also had Maxaret anti lock brakes and a 'Monolock' spin limiting system in the centre differential, effectively preventing more than 5 per cent overspin at the rear and 10 per cent at the front end, but allowing free inter axle rotation up to those limits. With such low power, no limited slip units were found necessary. That said, we shall never really know if its competitiveness was due to the relatively poor state of rear wheel drive GP car design, or a combination of the above factors. One must also consider that the behaviour of the front engined car when braking, accelerating (when the front tyres could be expected to do more work) and cornering with its 60/40 weight balance (dry) and very different mass distribution, which may have also influenced the result.

As history relates the Ferguson P99 (with 2½ litre Coventry Climax installed) and the BRM P67 driven by Peter Westbury and Peter Lawson respectively won RAC Hill Climb Championships, but again that was in an age before aerodynamic downforce and super wide tyres. As in the rally car case, the traction gain probably outweighed any handling disadvantage. Also, the handling requirements for narrow bumpy lanes are far more like those found on country roads and quite different from those of the average circuit where the car is sliding for a much longer period and at much higher speeds.

Aerodynamic downforce and tyre development may have saved RWD, but as things stand, my own view is that it would be difficult to imagine four wheel drive staging a comeback in Formula One or at Indianapolis (even if it were legal in either) if it were to involve a sacrifice in manoeuvrability. This suggests four wheel drive needs to be interfaced in a car designed to be highly manoeuvrable, (such as the Peugeot 16T rally car), to a point where the driver could not cope with the response in rear wheel drive form. In addition four wheel drive should not involve the imposition of a fixed torque bias as this has hitherto involved some sacrifice in driver control and handling response.

More sophisticated spin limiting devices such as the Ferguson developed viscous coupling, or Gleason differential should overcome some of the deficiencies present in earlier designs. Where the all important question of balance is concerned, new developments in active suspension and active steering also indicate that some form of artificial stability system could balance the car automatically according to the yaw response demanded by the driver. If all these systems could be incorporated without a weight penalty (which seems very unlikely) it might be possible to overcome some of the balance and manoeuvrability problems associated with four wheel drive and the race track.

Finally, it will be necessary to re-educate the driver in such a way that he is confident enough in the machine to cede years of conditioning that make him want to exercise final control over the balance of the car.

ACKNOWLEDGEMENTS

Bill Milliken (Milliken Res. Assoc.)
Doug Nye
Peter Wright (Lotus Cars Limited)
Ken Sears (Lotus Cars Limited)
Tony Rudd (Lotus Cars Limited)
Maurice Phillipe (Tyrrell Racing Org.)
Ken Tyrrell (Tyrrell Racing Org.)
Keith Duckworth (Cosworth Eng. Ltd.)
Tony Rolt (FF Developments Ltd.)
Mike Pilbeam (Pilbeam Racing Des. Ltd.)
Stirling Moss
Jackie Stewart
Dereck Bell
Mario Andretti

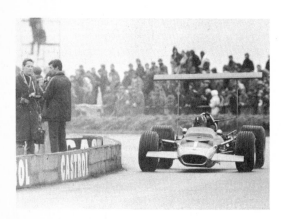

Fig 1   Graham Hill Lotus 49 (final development of wings) Silverstone 1969

Fig 2   Wing breakage on Lotus 49s leads to near fatal accidents at Barcelona 1969

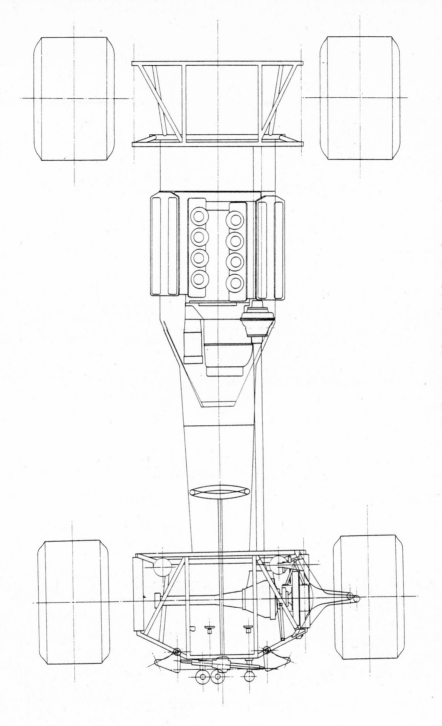

Fig 3   Lotus 63 — typical four by four

Fig 4   John Miles Lotus 63, 1969 British Grand Prix,
Silverstone

Fig 5   Cosworth four-wheel drive Grand Prix car

THE *FWD* AT PIKE'S PEAK

CONFIDENTIAL
· Report on the

PREPARATION AND PARTICIPATION OF THE
FOUR WHEEL DRIVE AUTO COMPANY'S
"FWD SPECIAL" IN THE 1948 ANNUAL
PIKE'S PEAK HILL CLIMB

With an examination of the technical
problems encountered in this competition.

by

W. F. Milliken, Jr.
January 1, 1949

Buffalo   New York

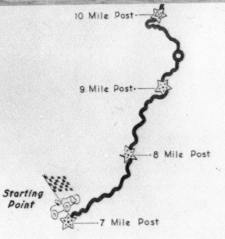

Fig 6   Bill Milliken four-wheel drive Miller, 1948, Pikes
Hill climb

Fig 7   Stirling Moss number 7 overtaking competitors, Oulton Park
Gold cup, 1961

Fig 8   R Drefus Bugatti T53, La Turbie Hill climb

C05/86

The influence of limited slip differentials on torque distribution and steady state handling of four-wheel drive military vehicles

L C HALL, BSc, MSc, CEng, MIMechE
Royal Military College of Science, Shrivenham, Swindon, Wiltshire

SYNOPSIS When limited slip differentials are fitted to a 4 WD vehicle the distribution of torque between the wheels during high speed cornering manoeuvres on roads can be complex. This influences the distribution of tractive effort and hence the handling of the vehicle in a manner which depends on the characteristics of the differentials fitted.

A suite of computer programs has been developed to predict the steady state handling behaviour of such vehicles, This paper reports the results of a study of the effect of fitting a variety of types of differential to a typical military reconnaissance vehicle.

1. INTRODUCTION

Wheeled armoured fighting vehicles are required to provide a high degree of off road mobility in addition to a high performance on roads to permit rapid deployment over large distances.

For ultimate soft ground mobility an all wheel drive transmission system without differentials (or with the differentials locked) is desirable. However operation on dry roads in this configuration results in unacceptably high wind-up torques in the transmission. The most common solution is to fit a differential on each axle with manual selection of single or all axle drive, sometimes with manually operated differential locks for severe conditions.

There are significant operational advantages in eliminating the requirement for manual intervention by providing a transmission system which automatically adapts to the terrain requirements. This usually involves fitting limited slip differentials of which there are several types on the market. Not only does each type operate on a different principle but it is often available with a range of different characteristics. A four wheeled vehicle with all wheel drive will require three differentials which need not be of the same type. The designer is therefore confronted with a bewildering range of options.

The choice of limited slip differentials for off road vehicles has usually been largely influenced by cross country mobility requirements. Interest in their effect on vehicle handling has grown in recent years with the advent of all wheel drive competition cars. The torque distribution in a vehicle fitted with limited slip differentials depends on the relative angular velocity of the wheels. This in turn is influenced by the effective rolling radius of the tyres and their peripheral velocity. The former depends on the tyre characteristics and the loads they carry whilst the latter depends on the trajectory kinematics the vehicle speed and the tyre longitudinal slip. Non uniform torque

distribution affects tractive effort distribution and contributes to the generation of significant yaw moments in addition to influencing tyre slip angles directly. Military off road vehicles can be more sensitive to these effects than passenger cars due to the requirement for a high ground clearance. This results in a high mass centre and hence large lateral and longitudinal weight transfers which cause significant changes in tyre effective rolling radii and hence in wheel angular velocities.

The selection and setting up of limited slip differentials using a trial and error approach is very time consuming and expensive, although in the final analysis practical trials are the only completely reliable method. In such situations a digital computer simulation can usually offer a means not only of speeding up this process but also of developing a deeper understanding of the problem. With this in mind a suite of computer programs has been developed at RMCS to simulate a four wheeled vehicle with all wheel drive. The programs have been designed to predict the distribution of torque in the transmission and hence the steady state handling of the vehicle in constant speed and constant radius cornering manoeuvres. The characteristics of the differentials can easily be altered so that comparisons can be made between different types. In addition the influence of a wide range of operating conditions, vehicle parameters and tyre characteristics can be readily examined.

2. LIMITED SLIP DIFFERENTIALS

A survey of limited slip differentials was carried out and they were categorised according to their operating principles under the following headings:

a) Free wheel.

In this type the entire torque is transferred to the more slowly rotating output shaft. The faster output shaft simply overruns.

b)   Constant friction bias.

The two output shafts are connected together by a preloaded friction clutch. If they rotate at different speeds the clutch slips thus transferring torque from the higher to the lower speed shaft.

c)   Torque sensitive bias.

In this type the magnitude of the torque transfer to the lower speed output shaft is a function of the differential input torque. The torque transfer is usually generated by friction as in b).

d)   Speed sensitive bias.

The torque transfer is a function of the difference in speed between the differential output shafts. This is usually achieved by means of a viscous coupling between them.

It was found that the characteristics of some differentials depended on combinations of the above principles. The simulation programs were designed to accommodate these more complex characteristics if required.

3.   STRUCTURE OF SIMULATION PROGRAMS

In limited slip differentials which rely on Coulomb friction to generate the torque transfer both output shafts will rotate at the same speed unless the torque difference between them exceeds the peak friction torque which can be sustained by the friction elements in the differential. Thus they can operate either in locked or unlocked modes. For a four wheeled vehicle fitted with three such differentials there are eight possible operating states. These are listed in Table 1.

Table 1   Transmission operating states

	Differential		
State	Inter axle	Front axle	Rear axle
1	U	U	U
2	L	U	U
3	U	L	U
4	U	U	L
5	L	L	U
6	U	L	L
7	L	U	L
8	L	L	L

L = locked   U = unlocked

Three Fortran simulation programs have been developed using techniques similar to those employed in ref 1. These correspond to states 1, 2 and 8 in Table 1.

3.1   Program DIFF

This program was designed to simulate the steady state handling behaviour of a two axle all wheel drive vehicle with three differentials all operating in the unlocked mode, i.e. state 1 in Table 1. In this state all wheels rotate at different angular velocities but the torque distribution is

determinate and depends on the characteristics of the differentials, which can easily be changed. The program uses iterative techniques to satisfy three equilibrium equations as follows.

i)   the total tractive effort developed by the tyres must equal the total resistance to motion plus the force required to accelerate the vehicle.

ii)   the total lateral force developed by the tyres must equal the product of vehicle mass and lateral acceleration plus the aerodynamic side force.

iii)   the yaw moment developed by the tyres must equal the aerodynamic yaw moment.

For a given speed and path curvature the program starts off by calculating the aerodynamic forces and moments assuming no wind. It then computes the four wheel loads taking account of both lateral and longitudinal weight transfer. The trajectory kinematics are then analysed to determine the velocity and slip angle at each wheel station based on initial estimates of the front and rear axle slip angles. This permits an initial estimate of the driveline angular velocities and the torque input to the inter axle differential.

This torque is then distributed between the four wheels in a manner depending on the characteristics of the differentials being modelled. The traction at each wheel is then estimated.

At this point a tyre subroutine is called. This calculates the effective rolling radius, the peak adhesion coefficient, the cornering stiffness, the self aligning torque, the longitudinal stiffness coefficient and the rolling resistance of each tyre. It then uses iteration to determine the longitudinal slip necessary to generate the required tractive force and from this it determines the lateral force developed.

Returning to the main program the total tractive effort is computed and compared with the resistance to motion. The driveline input torque is then stepped iteratively until the two balance. The lateral force equation is then examined and balanced by stepping the front and rear axle slip angles by equal amounts. Finally the yaw moment equation is balanced by applying steps of equal magnitude but opposite sign to the front and rear axle slip angles. Eventually the simulation converges on the equilibrium condition and the steady state conditions are printed out.

3.2   Program NODIFF

Consider a vehicle fitted with Coulomb friction biased limited slip differentials in which the effective rolling radii of all the tyres is the same. When driven in a straight line all differentials will be locked. If the vehicle now starts to turn the differentials will remain locked until the torque difference generated by tyre longitudinal slip on any differential exceeds the friction torque. Until this point all wheels will rotate at the same angular velocity and the torque distribution will depend on tyre characteristics and the trajectory kinematics. This is the state (8 in Table 1) which is simulated by program NODIFF.

The program uses iteration to satisfy the same three equations as program DIFF but starts off with an estimate of driveline angular velocity instead of input torque. No iteration is necessary in the tyre subroutine and the total tractive effort is balanced against the resistance to motion by stepping the driveline angular velocity. The lateral force and yaw moment equations are handled as explained in section 3.1.

3.3 Program DIFFLOK

In a normal cornering situation the difference in angular velocity between inner and outer wheels on each axle is of a similar magnitude and much greater than that between front and rear axles. If the vehicle is fitted with friction biased limited slip differentials the axle differentials will unlock at a much larger radius of turn than the inter axle differential. The vehicle will then spend a significant amount of time in state 2 (see Table 1).

This program was designed to simulate vehicle behaviour with the inter axle differential locked. It can accept different characteristics for the front and rear axle differentials. The program is broadly similar to DIFF but has to satisfy a fourth equilibrium equation i.e. that the inter axle differential output shaft angular velocities must be equal. This is achieved by introducing an extra loop in which the inter axle differential output torques are stepped by amounts of equal magnitude but of opposite sign until convergence of output shaft speeds takes place.

4. DETAILS OF THE VEHICLE MODEL

A specification was drawn up for a reference vehicle as shown in Table 2. The data given are typical of an armoured reconnaissance vehicle.

4.1 Tyres

The behaviour of the tyres was predicted by a tyre subroutine designed to model their characteristics using methods described by Dugoff et al in ref 2. The input data for the model were derived from experimental results for 11.00 - 20 military run flat tyres generated by Hooke (ref 3) using the RMCS tyre test facility. An inflation pressure of 25 lbf/in^2 was chosen for front and rear tyres which gave a static load of about 15.3 kN for the recommended on-road deflection of 13.5% of section height.

Empirical equations for tyre cornering stiffness, effective rolling radius, longitudinal stiffness and coefficient of adhesion as functions of tyre load plus self aligning torque as a function of slip angle were taken directly from ref. 3. The tyre rolling resistance coefficient was assumed to be 0.018 and the effect of slip angle α on this parameter was taken into account by introducing a factor of $(1 + 300 \alpha^2)$ where α is measured in radians. This was based on data extracted from ref 4 and on measurements made at RMCS.

4.2 Suspension and steering systems

The suspension units were assumed to be identical at each wheel station using transverse links and coil springs. The model was designed to take account of wheel camber in roll, steering system compliance and suspension jacking effects. The steering system was assumed to conform to the Ackermann model but the simulation could easily be modified to accept the characteristics of real systems.

Table 2. Reference vehicle specification

Vehicle

Total mass	6240	kg
Wheelbase	2.4	m
Track	1.75	m
Height of mass centre	1.0	m
Frontal area	1.2	m^2
Drag coefficient	1.0	
Height of aerodynamic centre of pressure	1.2	m
Aerodynamic side force coefficient gradient	-2.0	rad^{-1}
Aerodynamic yaw moment coefficient gradient	-0.3	rad^{-1}

Suspension

Unsprung mass (per wheelstation)	312	kg
Wheel rate (per wheelstation)	96	kN/m
Jacking rate (per axle)	200	kN/m
Roll stiffness (per axle)	150	kN m/rad
Camber rate in roll	0.3	
Roll centre height	0.43	m
Static wheel camber	0.02	rad

Steering system

Steering gear ratio	20
Kingpin offset	0.06 m
Kingpin inclination	0.16 rad
Caster angle	0.02 rad

Tyres

Size	11.00 - 20
Undeflected radius	0.535 m
Inflation pressure	25 lbf/in^2
Radial stiffness	540 kN/m

4.3 Transmission system

The transmission system was assumed to comprise two axle differentials, an inter axle differential and hub reduction gearboxes laid out as shown in fig 1. Transmission losses were estimated on the basis of 2% for each pair of gears when operated at their rated torque. Half of this loss was assumed to be load dependent, the remainder constant.

Four different types of differential were modelled as follows

a) Free differentials in which equal torques are delivered by the output shafts.

b) Constant friction bias differentials in which the torque transfer is assumed to be 300 Nm at the inter axle differential and 200 Nm at the front and rear axles.

c) Torque sensitive differentials in which the torque transfer was assumed to be 25% of the input torque. This gives an output torque ratio of 3:1.

d) Viscous differentials in which the torque transfer (N) is given by K (output shaft speed difference)$^{0.6}$ where K is 100 for the inter axle differential and 50 for the front and rear axle differentials, the speed difference being expressed in rad/s.

4.4 Vehicle operating conditions

The steady state handling of the reference vehicle was predicted under conditions of zero gradient on a wet pavement assuming a coefficient of adhesion of 0.53 at the tyre static load. The vehicle speed was assumed constant and lateral acceleration was varied by stepping the radius of turn.

In order to examine the influence of throttle position on handling the simulation was repeated with torque inputs to the inter axle differential of 3000 Nm and -500 Nm. These values, referred to the wheel angular velocity, were estimated to be consistent with full throttle and overrun conditions respectively. For these runs the conditions were assumed to be quasi steady state.

5. RESULTS AND DISCUSSION

The results presented in this paper are limited to predictions of the behaviour of the reference vehicle specified in Table 2 when fitted with differentials of identical types at front, rear and between the axles whilst executing cornering manoeuvres at a constant speed of 60 km/h.

5.1 Free differentials

Figure 2 shows the predicted handling characteristic of the vehicle when fitted with free differentials. These are assumed to have zero torque bias whereas in practice a small amount would be present. Despite having the mass centre at mid wheelbase, identical tyres and suspension units at each wheelstation and the torque equally distributed between the wheels the vehicle exhibits a marked understeer characteristic. The understeer coefficient is about 1.3 at low lateral accelerations rising to give terminal understeer as lateral acceleration increases. This is due to the development of an increasing understeering yaw moment resulting from the combined effects of tyre self aligning torques and traction transfer to the inside wheels. The latter is a consequence of the effect of lateral weight transfer, which in this vehicle is substantial, on tyre rolling resistance. This becomes very significant at the large slip angles which are generated at high lateral accelerations. This increase in rolling resistance is reflected in the rising wheel torques shown in fig 2.

The influence of throttle position on handling behaviour appears to be negligible at low lateral accelerations but becomes noticeable at high values where torque levels are higher. Fig 2 shows typical lift-off oversteer behaviour which is associated with longitudinal weight transfer.

5.2 Constant friction bias differentials

At low lateral accelerations the radius of turn is very large, and when the wind-up torque in the transmission is insufficient to overcome the friction in the differentials the transmission will be solid with all wheels rotating at the same angular velocity. For this condition program NODIFF predicts the behaviour shown in fig 3. The vehicle exhibits a strong understeer characteristic with an understeer coefficient of about 2.5 at low lateral accelerations and the wind-up torque across the front and rear differentials rises sharply with lateral acceleration.

When the constant friction bias differentials are fitted as soon as the wind-up torque across the axle differentials reaches a value of 400 Nm it is sufficient to unlock them. This occurs at a lateral acceleration of approximately 0.5 - 0.6 m/s^2, the front axle differential unlocking first to give transmission state 7 (see Table 1). The inter axle differential remains locked until a lateral acceleration of about 2.7 m/s^2 is reached.

The predicted vehicle behaviour is shown in figure 4. When driven in a straight line a small traction transfer is evident to the front axle resulting from a rearward weight transfer due to aerodynamic effects. Up to a lateral acceleration of 0.6 m/s^2 the torque distribution alters rapidly, transfer taking place from outside to inside wheels. Above this value lateral torque transfer remains constant at 200 Nm but the general level of torque in the transmission increases with increasing resistance to motion. At the same time the longitudinal torque transfer increases steadily largely due to trajectory kinematic effects.

The unlocking of the front and rear differentials causes a sharp drop in understeer coefficient to a value of about 1.3. This rises with lateral acceleration to give terminal understeer at around 3.5 m/s^2. Lift off oversteer is still apparent but not to a significantly greater extent than that of the same vehicle fitted with free differentials.

5.3 Torque sensitive differentials

Not surprisingly the general pattern of behaviour of the vehicle when fitted with torque sensitive differentials was found to be similar to that with constant friction bias differentials. However the lateral acceleration at which the front and rear differentials unlock is now dependent on the level of torque input to the differentials, which would be determined by throttle position. Under constant speed zero gradient conditions it happens at about 0.3 m/s^2. Once the axle differentials unlock the torque transfers at front and rear now increase with lateral acceleration as a result of the increasing throttle opening required to overcome the rolling resistance. (See fig 5). The inter axle differential remains locked at all lateral accelerations.

The handling characteristics become much more sensitive to throttle position due to the influence of torque on the bias of the axle differentials. At full throttle all differentials remain locked until the lateral acceleration reaches about 1 m/s^2 and the cornering appears to be limited by understeer to about 3 m/s^2. A sizeable gap appears between the constant speed and overrun steer angle characteristics indicating a considerable degree of lift off oversteer which will require substantial steer correction at high lateral accelerations.

5.4 Viscous differentials

The torque transfers generated by the viscous differentials when the vehicle corners at 60 km/h are relatively small since the speed differences imposed on the differential output shafts are small, particularly at the inter axle differential. Fig 6 shows how these differences vary with lateral acceleration and it should be noted that they will also be directly influenced by vehicle speed. The speed difference across the axle differentials increases with lateral acceleration up to about 2.5 m/s^2 but beyond that the angular velocity of the inner wheels begins to increase due to the large lateral and traction forces imposed on the tyres in relation to the reducing normal load. In addition the front outer wheel begins to slow down due to a combination of lateral weight transfer and a large slip angle at the front axle. This generates a very high rolling resistance which eventually exceeds the traction applied to the wheel. As a result of these effects the lateral torque transfers reduce as shown in fig 7.

The handling characteristic is similar to that of the vehicle fitted with free differentials and shows a similarly low sensitivity to throttle position with only a small degree of lift off oversteer.

5.5 Handwheel torque

The simulation programs also calculate the moments generated about the king pin axes and hence the handwheel torque. This ignores any friction in the steering mechanism but includes both caster and tyre self aligning torques as well as front wheel traction moments about the king pin. In practice of course a vehicle of this type would probably have power assisted steering.

Fig 8 shows the predicted influence of lateral acceleration on handwheel torque during constant speed cornering at 60 km/h. It is clear that the torque transfer generated by fitting a limited slip differential to the front axle makes the steering heavier. The viscous differential, as might be expected, has the least effect. Those relying on a Coloumb friction bias show once again a discontinuity at the point where the front axle differential unlocks, which occurs at a lateral acceleration of 0.6 m/s^2 with the constant friction bias differential. At lower values of lateral acceleration the hand wheel torque follows the upper curve in fig 8 which is the predicted behaviour with all differentials locked. When the torque sensitive differential is fitted to the front axle the handwheel torque is sensitive to throttle position.

5.6 General observations

The results presented in this paper are for a constant speed of 60 km/h and for a vehicle with a static weight distribution of 50/50 front/rear. Clearly at higher speeds at the same lateral acceleration the relative angular velocities of inner and outer wheels will be greater. Adjustments to weight distribution will also affect these velocities, although the effects may be compensated by changes in tyre inflation

pressures. Therefore if these conditions are changed there is likely to be some effect on the torque distribution in the transmission and hence the handling behaviour of the vehicle.

The choice of characteristics for the limited slip differentials used to obtain the results presented in this paper was of necessity somewhat arbitrary but they were judged to be typical for the type of vehicle considered. Clearly the results would be significantly changed if different characteristics were used.

In the interests of simplicity the results presented in this paper have been for a vehicle with identical types of differential throughout. In practice it is common to fit one type to the axles and a different type between them. Furthermore front and rear differentials, even though of the same type, may well have different characteristics.

It has been found that under some circumstances the vehicle can operate over a significant range of lateral accelerations in state 7 as defined in Table 1. An additional simulation program will be required to deal with this situation.

Although the predictions of these programs give useful insight into the behaviour of this type of vehicle caution should be exercised in translating the results to a real vehicle. It must be remembered that the tyre model, even though based on laboratory measurements, can only provide approximate predictions of behaviour, particularly at high values of lateral and longitudinal force generation. Furthermore several influences have been ignored in generating the results presented here, for example roll steer and toe in, steering system compliance and actual steering system geometry. These effects can however be incorporated into the simulation if required.

No attempt has been made to model the transient behaviour of the vehicle. This would require data on the transient characteristics of the tyres and simulation of the transient torques in the transmission system. There is very little information available on either topic for vehicles of this type.

6. CONCLUSIONS

For a high mobility 4 x 4 armoured vehicle with the static weight equally divided between the wheels and fitted with 1100-20 run flat tyres:

6.1 The fitting of limited slip differentials will affect the torque distribution when the vehicle negotiates a corner with zero gradient on roads and lead to an increase in understeer.

6.2 If a differential which relies on Coulomb friction for torque biasing is installed between the axles it tends to remain locked during high speed cornering on wet roads.

6.3 If differentials which rely on Coulomb friction for torque biasing are fitted to front and rear axles they tend to remain locked at low lateral accelerations. When they unlock a sudden drop in understeer coefficient is predicted.

6.4 When equipped with viscous differentials the steady state handling characteristics do not appear to be very different than when free differentials are fitted.

6.5 Torque sensitive differentials appear to generate greater lift off oversteer effects than the other types examined.

7. REFERENCES

1. HALL, L.C. "The influence of transmission torques on the steady state handling of all wheel drive vehicles having one transverse differential".
Road Vehicle Handling, MEP, London 1983 pp 129-138 Paper No C122/83

2. DUGOFF, H, FANCHER, P.S. and SEGEL, L. "An analysis of tire traction properties and their influence on vehicle dynamic performance".
SAE Transactions 1970
Paper No 700377

3. HOOKE, C.J. "Handling simulation of CVR(W)"
MSc Project Report No 2/12 MVT. RMCS 1984

4. RAMSHAW, J. and WILLIAMS, T. "The rolling resistance of commercial vehicle tyres"
TRRL Supplementary Report 701, 1981.

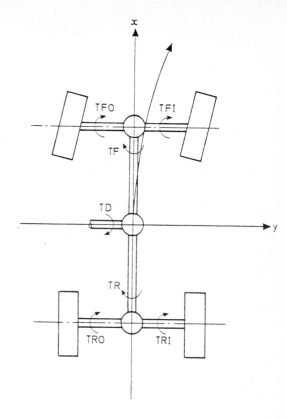

T = Torque	D = Drive
F = Front	I = Inner
R = Rear	O = Outer

Fig 1   Transmission system layout

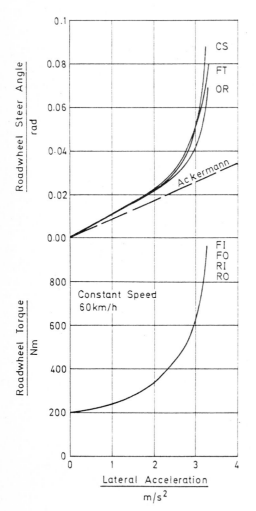

CS = Constant Speed   F = Front   I = Inner
FT = Full Throttle   R = Rear   O = Outer
OR = Overrun

Fig 2   Free differentials

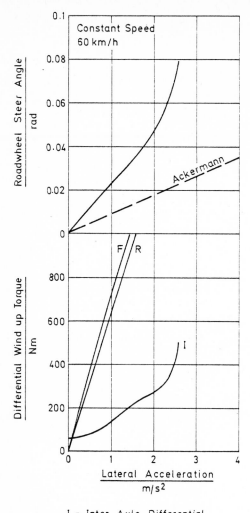

I = Inter Axle Differential
F = Front Axle Differential
R = Rear Axle Differential

Fig 3   All differentials locked

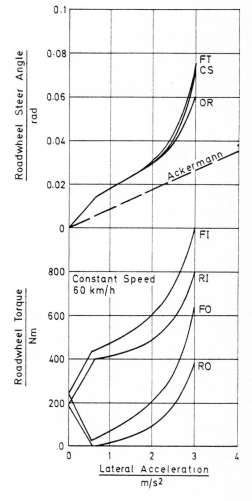

CS = Constant Speed   F = Front   I = Inner
FT = Full Throttle   R = Rear   O = Outer
OR = Overrun

Fig 4   Constant friction bias differentials

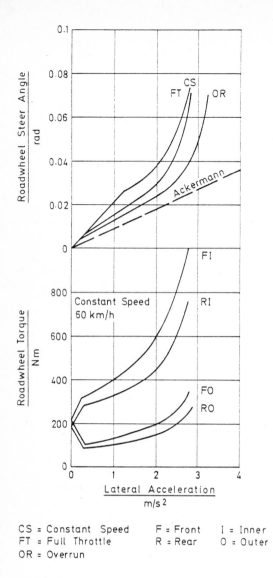

CS = Constant Speed   F = Front   I = Inner
FT = Full Throttle   R = Rear   O = Outer
OR = Overrun

Fig 5   Torque sensitive differentials (3 : 1 torque ratio)

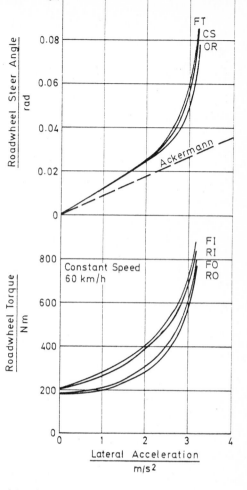

CS = Constant Speed   F = Front   I = Inner
FT = Full Throttle   R = Rear   O = Outer
OR = Overrun

Fig 7   Viscous differentials

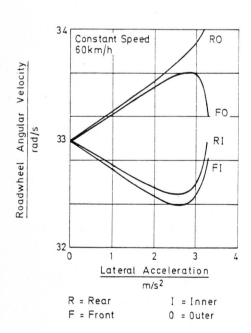

R = Rear   I = Inner
F = Front   0 = Outer

Fig 6   Road wheel angular velocities with viscous differentials

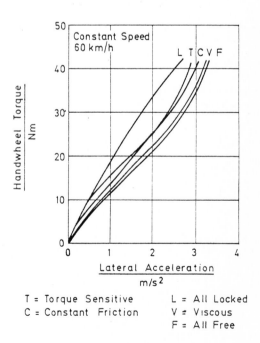

T = Torque Sensitive   L = All Locked
C = Constant Friction   V = Viscous
                         F = All Free

Fig 8   Hand wheel torques

C03/86

Four-wheel drive – a customer's viewpoint

J STAZIKER, CEng, MIMechE
North Western Electricity Board, Manchester

SYNOPSIS   A limited market reduces choice in terms of capacity, performance, options and
price, and customers must accept 'conversions'.   Most 4-W-D vehicles are equipped for
special duties and many provide on-site power for equipment carried, such as hydraulic
platforms, winches and powered tools.

Specifications and operating costs are discussed together with their operational and
quantitive implications.   A requirement for a 5-6 tonne is outlined and specification
priorities identified.   Can commercial operators use the emerging 4-W-D cars and what
are their limitations?   Hopefully the development of 'world wide' vehicles will provide
improved transmissions, prices and choice but continuing interest in their special
applications.

1   INTRODUCTION

It is unlikely that there are many
Commercial vehicle operators who
require all-wheel drive-trains to
enhance road performance or handling
characteristics and the main reason
for specifying these must be to
improve effective tractive effort,
sometimes when weight distribution
is not ideal.   All-wheel drive is an
advantage where high powered
tractors are used to haul very heavy
trailers as it is for snow clearing
vehicles, but the most common reason
for seeking better traction occurs
where it is necessary to improve the
chances of load carrying vehicles
reaching off-road sites all year
round.   I do not see the all-wheel
drive vehicle generally being in
competition with tracked, low ground
pressure vehicles because these do
not have road mobility.

Apart from military uses the requirement arises over a wide range of
activities in the agricultural,
forestry, construction and service
industries and whilst the ratio of
4-W-D to two wheel drive vehicles
reflects the location of work sites
and contingency policies, it also
relates to operating costs and sometimes the limited choice of suitable
4-W-D vehicles.   Obviously if total
operating costs were similar without
any significant loss in pay-load,
performance or reliability, 4-W-D
units could outnumber the rest.
Quantatively then the over-riding
constraint is that of operating
costs and this paper discusses a
customer's requirements and purchasing decisions relative to this.

2   4-W-D APPLICATIONS AND SPECIFI-CATIONS

In the energy supply, telecommunications and water industries most
vehicles are assigned and equipped,
for special purposes and often serve
as an on-site power source for
special equipment.   In some cases
the basic vehicle forms but a part
of the final capital investment, and
equipment having a high added value
can include hydraulic work platforms, drilling equipment and many
types of purpose built bodies specified for maintenance or emergency
services.   Because of their specialist nature it is not practicable to
deploy vehicles on a day to day
basis to cope with work site
locations or road conditions at the
time and in practice a decision must
be taken when initiating a specification whether 4-W-D drive is
essential or justified on the
balance of cost and operational
conditions likely to be experienced
over the life of the vehicle.

For example, Figure 1 illustrates a
requirement to provide a powerful
winching service for the erection
and tensioning of high voltage over-
head conductors.   The outline specification included the need for high
mobility as well as off-road performance to enable the winch quickly to
reach grid-line locations up to 200
kilometers from base should a
failure occur.   The final positioning of the winch often necessitates
overcoming difficult off-road
terrain to gain access to steel
tower positions in hill country and
in some conditions a low ground

pressure tracked vehicle would perform better. However, in this case a good road performance was the compelling reason for choosing the Unimog 'U900' which with its 'stepped' drive-axles, good ground clearance and tyre spread provides the off-road performance expected. To allow tensioning loads of up to 6 tonnes a ground anchor is included at the rear of the chassis and the Plumett TL80 hydraulic winch also incorporates a dynamometer to record the tension applied, together with a sophisticated 'failsafe' braking system. The anchor is powered by the vehicle's standard, crankshaft driven, hydraulic service system and drive for the winch hydrostatic transmission is taken from the transfer-box power take-off with a maximum power demand of about 55kW.

The total investment of £53,000 includes a chassis cost of £21,000 and with other standing and running costs a charge of £200 per day is necessary when utilisation may be no more than 30 days a year. This high cost is acceptable because no compromise in performance can be contemplated when related to power supply shut-down costs where, for example, revenue losses alone of up to £2,500 an hour may be faced together with unfavourable customer reactions.

Not all telecommunications and low voltage electricity pole mounted lines are distanced from hard surfaced roads or forestry roads but 4-W-D is essential for reliable year round access. A typical specification for a 'line' construction team vehicle can include accommodation for up to 4 men and facilities to carry tools and equipment together with consumable materials. Various ladders and even tubular pole erection derricks up to 6 metres in length are to be found on roof racks and roof loadings up to 200kg are not unusual. A towing capability is usually needed to draw trailers carrying further material such as conductor cable both on and off-road. This specification can be met by quantity produced bonneted vehicles such as the '110' Land Rover which is adequate and cost effective for a 2 man team but where more men need to be carried, accommodation and load carrying space are limited. Larger military derived chassis in the 10 to 16 tonne gross vehicle weight range can be considered but may be ruled out not only on cost grounds but because of their weight and turning circle. Frequently vehicles need to operate on and access through privately owned land and narrow lanes where the good

will and acceptance of the land owner is important. Because suitable purpose built 4-W-D vehicles in the 3 to 4 tonne gross vehicle weight range are not available, one solution is to utilise orthodox commercial chassis and vans converted to 4-W-D by specialists.

Figure 2 shows a conversion of the Bedford 'CF350' van that includes permanent 4-W-D with a central controlled slip differential and asymmetric torque distribution system and in this example the fitment of 16" wheels to improve ground clearance. The 7.50 x 16 tyres effectively increased the final drive ratio by 24% which unfortunately could not fully be compensated for due to the limited availability of optional axle ratio from the chassis manufacturers. Later versions were, therefore, specified with 205 x 16 tyres resulting in a more acceptable compromise as between ground clearance and transmission ratio. Except in very difficult terrain and construction site conditions ground clearance need not always be equal to that required for military purposes and in fact lower chassis heights may be preferred so as to reduce loading and load centre heights. Reduced chassis height increases the risk of grounding but the addition of guards to vulnerable components such as fuel tanks and engine sumps can provide some protection and on occasion can at least produce scraping noises as a warning to the unwary driver.

In the light-weight vehicle range weight distribution tolerances are often limited with both converted and purpose-built chassis and where a drum type winch is required as was the case with the Bedford van, a front mounting position can result in marginal front axle load when the vehicle carries a full pay-load. Battery- powered winches, however, have the virtue of installation simplicity, and in this case a 1500kg winch was initially mounted suspended between the chassis at the rear but in a later version a location inside the van immediately behind a central bulkhead gave a less costly and better protected position. The severity of off-road conditions vary widely and some customers may have reservations about using converted commercial vans but my experience has been that drivers and maintenance staff have been satisfied with no evidence of over-stressing of the chassis or body structures although the fitting of a central bulkhead no doubt contributes to the torsional stiffness of the van body. Conversion costs of £4,000 result in a total cost of £11,900 excluding fitting out costs and a vehicle life of 6 or 7 years is planned.

Vehicle mounted hydraulic work platforms often need to be mounted on a 4-W-D chassis and present interesting problems of stability limits in the fully extended working position, when fitted to light-weight chassis. As can be seen from Figure 3 the platform in the closed position is virtually designed around the profile of the chassis/cab and hence allows very limited scope to position the base mounting to obtain the optimum weight distribution. Chassis mounted support jacks assist in maintaining transverse stability but on relatively short wheel-base chassis stability in the longitudinal axle may be more critical. This particular version, however, provides a good value for money package with good manoeuvreability and a platform working height of up to 9 metres, although with a 2 man crew the remaining payload is limited to about 220kg.

3   STANDING COSTS

In assessing operating costs the initial purchase price and resulting depreciation charges form the major part of standing charges and Table 1 compares prices of a range of vehicles. The two-wheel drive versions are paired where possible with similar or identical vehicles and the comparison illustrates that the additional cost of 4-W-D varies from 23% in the saloon car range to 75% for a 16 tonne 'gross' chassis. This variation may reflect production volumes and design origins but probably also a little of what the market will bear. Certainly when a pay-load of upwards of 10 tonnes is needed a customer seems to get much more for his money from a 6 x 4 vehicle than he does from a 4-W-D model and the loss in tractive effort is relatively small when 75% of the weight may be carried on driven wheels.

The excavator is included to illustrate a type of mechanically driven wheeled plant primarily used as a site vehicle that is also available with 4-W-D. Sales of the 4-W-D version of this particular model built up over a four year period to an unexpected level of 50% for a machine which is traditionally expected to 'walk' its way out of trouble using the front and rear mounted excavating equipment. It seems more likely the preference is because of its developing use for off-road mechanical handling applications. Its emergence, however, may owe much to the effects of keen international competition which generally has the effect of providing the customer with a wider choice of options than would otherwise be available.

In assessing depreciation charges the 4-W-D vehicle, at least in the light-weight category, does have the advantage of allowing a longer service life together with a predictable and reliable disposal value that can extend to 10 years or more if need be.

The comparison of depreciation costs in Table 2, suggest that with a 10 year life the annual cost of £687 can be similar to that for a typical 1 Tonne van over an 8 year life. The better residual values of the 4-W-D is influenced by its more durable construction as well as the demand from 'private' buyers who may often keep them in service up to 20 years. 'Sighting' a Land Rover in a scrap-yard is indeed a rare experience but may be, like elephants, their life ends in a remote and secret place.

4   RUNNING COSTS

Running costs must also be considered when making the purchasing decision and Table 2 compares average maintenance and fuel costs as between the Land Rover and an orthodox van of similar capacity. The particular models were chosen only because it was possible to obtain average costs from a fairly large sample size. It is always hazardous to compare maintenance costs when labour charges may include workshop overheads to varying degrees but the costs in the examples derive from similar gross labour charges and maintenance routines. In comparing costs it must be borne in mind that the 4-W-D vehicles incur added repair costs because of increased wear and tear in off-road conditions to which normal road vehicles are not subjected. This can sometimes include prolonged use of the engine and power take-offs to operate other equipment and often some if not all of the cost of maintaining this equipment finds its way into the vehicle repair account. Obviously a more complex drive train results in some added costs in maintaining drive shaft joints and seals, etc, but there seems little evidence that component failures are due to inadequate design rather than driver misuse. I suggest that few customers would feel that these extra costs are in themselves significant.

For similar operational reasons fuel costs are bound to be higher and relative to the proportion of off-road and low gear progress on difficult roads. Also the traditional and heavier 4-W-D vehicle rarely has an exciting drag-factor which is not improved by the presence of roof mounted equipment. In the fleet costs compared, petrol rather than diesel engines were preferred because of the relatively low mileage which results in a break-even total cost point not being reached until late in the five or six year life of the vehicle. The added cost of the diesel engine option is, of course, the most important factor in this but the comparative engine power and torque characteristics are another particularly when trailer work may be necessary. If the diesel engine does not provide adequate torque then the driver has to resort to frequent use of lower gears to develop the necessary power with the consequent effect on fuel consumption and engine service life.

5   QUANTATIVE PURCHASING DECISIONS

Reference was made earlier to the reasons for specifying 4-W-D but perhaps these could be expanded a little together with the cost relationships. This may best be illustrated by discussing requirements in two categories:

(i)   Where 4-W-D performance is essential to avoid unacceptable access delays in the continuity of work.

(ii) Where it is desirable for other vehicles which may have to support the specialist vehicles at certain times particularly as a contingency measure to cope with winter snow covered ground and access roads.

The first category may seem to be the simplest to meet since it appears to be merely a question of supplying the most suitable 'value for money' vehicle to meet the capacity and performance needed but there can nevertheless be a limit to an acceptable price since there may be another solution. For example, where the requirement is for say, a 2-3 tonne pay-load crew vehicle this can alternatively be met by providing a 1 tonne 4-W-D vehicle together with a conventional 2 tonne factory produced van. The larger van then serves as a materials carrier and mobile base with the smaller vehicle meeting the off-road demands. Running costs must be considered but even though the arrangement has the added virtue of allowing the crew to

split into two groups if need be, it is a cost related practice that is far from ideal which would be changed given the right 4-W-D vehicle at the right price.

Quantatively the second category is related to operational judgements strongly influenced by vehicle cost but also by the effect a 4-W-D specification may perhaps have on comparative carrying capacity and performance, together with driver acceptance since for most of the time it is in use solely as a road vehicle. Local operating conditions are known but long range winter weather conditions are not and operational management is much more inclined to invest in more 4-W-D vehicles following two successive bad winters than it is after one mild one. Snow storm damaged transmission lines, for example, have quickly to be restored and the effectiveness in organising resources is critically dependant on good communications and the availability of 4-W-D vehicles to reach as close as possible to the trouble spot where it can not only support the work but act as a telecommunications point.

Ambulance services must also continue on untreated or uncleared winter roads and 4-W-D versions form a part of many fleets. These cannot merely be held in reserve and performance comparisons particularly of suspension systems and the effects on passenger and patient comfort as well as cost are constraints in arriving at the right complement of vehicles for the location.

6   A FOUR-WHEEL DRIVE LIGHT-MIDDLEWEIGHT

I believe most customers provided with the opportunities of this conference would wish to put forward ideas on a vehicle specification aimed at meeting their own particular needs and I cannot overlook the chance. There appears to be an adequate and widening choice of 4-W-D vehicles available of the car-related and purpose designed types with load carrying capacities up to 1 tonne and various passenger carrying arrangements. A limited choice of military derived chassis is also available in the 12 to 16 tonne gross weight class together with 'conversions' in the middleweight range.

Manufacturers seem, however, largely to have ignored the 2 to 3 tonne pay-load class and Figure 4 illustrates a suggested vehicle that might attract customers in a number of fields. The outline drawing profiles a chassis which might be achieved by utilising equal capacity axles of 3 tonnes and nominal 16 inch wheels. A forward control cab with a 3.4 metre wheel-base chassis should allow a body or load length of up to 3 metres and an axle track of 1.8 metres a body width of 2.1 metres. A good load centre tolerance would result if a gross vehicle weight of about 5.2 tonnes was aimed at. To provide for the fitting of open front access bodies of varied height and for extended crew-cabs there is a need for a cab which would tolerate the removal of or be supplied without a rear panel. Increasingly customer and body-builders prefer to construct a body to a complete cab rather than a chassis-cawl so as to provide a cab area with trim, seating, and fittings equal to factory produced levels. Body mounting arrangements need to be compatible with the cab mountings and perhaps a complete floor-pan is a feasible option so as to ensure this.

To allow for customers preferences in wheel and tyre sizes and perhaps engine options, 3 or 4 final-drive ratio options ought to be available. If these are necessary in 2 wheel drive specifications, as they seem to be, then they ought equally to be available in the 4-W-D field. In this category of vehicle perhaps permanent 4 wheel drive would provide the design advantage of lower drive shaft torque loadings and whether the drive-ratio options are provided from the transfer-box or axle is a matter of design or production preference.

An air over hydraulic braking system would ease the problem of providing a power braking system for heavy trailers and in addition to transmission power take-off facilities a direct drive from the engine crank-shaft is often also needed or preferred. This requires a radiator position to allow a drive shaft to be taken forward but ought to be feasible with a cross-flow type.

A forward control cab particularly cannot be designed to accommodate a very wide range of engines from a space point of view but maybe it is realistic to expect that customers' preferences could now be met by a 4 cylinder diesel engine, turbo charged to provide varying outputs.

I am not qualified to forecast total market potential for a vehicle of this capacity or possible military interest but even if the total requirement is relatively small a manufacturer may find it more profitable to take the opportunity rather than achieve a small percentage of the sales in a more competitive range. Price would obviously relate to volume but a level of say, 25 to 30 per cent above an equivalent 2 wheel drive version would be very acceptable.

7   FUTURE DEVELOPMENTS

The concept of the design and development of vehicles for a world-wide market ought to provide many benefits and useful technical innovation to 4-W-D customers and importantly result in a wider choice of vehicles and options. Perhaps the idea of extending engine management devices to provide transmission management is not too fancyful when tractive effort would only be directed to a wheel that signals its ability to accept it. This would ultimately necessitate limiting power output in certain conditions as with controlled braking and maybe an integrated sensing system is possible. In the meantime better warning devices and aids to prevent over-use of differential locks would be welcome. Not all drivers take an interest in the techniques to obtain the best off-road performance and in any case may be recruited and assessed for important skills other than driving. In this respect training courses on off-road driving techniques when provided by manufacturers are a welcome service and have more impact than 'in house' training methods.

The ever increasing number of cars and lightweight pick-ups available with 4-W-D option may create limited interest in commercial fleets particularly for occasional off-road uses and where the price is attractive. These appear to have emerged to create a market rather than to meet a particular demand and it would be interesting to see this approach extended into the light-medium weight field. Customers will need to look closely at ground clearance, and the vulnerability of under-chassis components to damage, particularly exposed drive-shafts, steering linkage and engine sumps where these are not re-positioned or protected.

I am often invited to contribute to vehicle market research programmes but never as yet in the 4-W-D field. This may indicate that research is limited or perhaps recognition that the usual techniques are not valid when customer specification priorities are so varied. Direct contact between producers and as wide a range of customers as possible at the design concept stage is probably the most satisfying method. Where ever production may centre in the future it is hoped that

manufacturers recognise the
importance of providing design and
evaluation support for the host of
special equipment added to many
4-W-D vehicles. May the
'applications' engineer be ever
enthusiastic in his involvement, and
respected in his judgements and
always, may he be available.

Table 1

Vehicle price comparisons

Model	Pay-load (kg)	Cost (£) 2WD	4WD	Added Cost (%)
Bedford 250 van	1,160	5,683	–)	41
Land Rover 110	1,273	–	8,020)	
Sherpa 250 van	1,295 ≠	5,484	8,639	57
Bedford 350 van	1,911 ≠	7,926	11,926	50
Bedford KB26 p/u	1,205	4,831	–)	30
Bedford KB4 p/u	1,140	–	6,278)	
Bedford TL1000	5,798	13,800	–)	33
Bedford MJR1	6,460	–	18,348)	
Bedford TL1630	11,600	20,375	–)	75
Bedford TM4-4	10,400	–	35,809)	
Bedford TL2440	18,500	27,270 (6 x 4)		
Fiat 'Panda'	4 seats	3,644	4,545	25
Subaru 1-8 GLS	4 seats	7,299	9,000	23
JCB 3CX Excavator	1,000	22,750	25,650	12

≠ 2 wheel drive version

Table 2

Depreciation Costs

	Land Rover 109 (110) H/Top			Bedford '250' van		
	Value (£)	Loss in Value (%)	Dep'n (£)	Value (£)	Loss in Value (%)	Dep'n (£)
New	8,020	–	–	5,683	–	–
3 years	2,500	69	1,840	1,250	78	1,477
5 years	1,950	76	1,214	700	88	996
8 years	1,400	83	827	200	96	685
10 years	1,150	86	687	–	–	–

(Source – Glass's Guide, Nov, 85)

Table 3

Maintenance and fuel costs

Vehicle	109 Land Rover		1 Tonne Van	
	(Fleet 1)	(Fleet 2)	(Fleet 1)	(Fleet 2)
Sample Size	88	95	227	378
Average miles/year	6,700	8,600	7,400	7,000
Maint (per year)	£722	£840	£464	£414
Costs (per mile)	10.6p	9.7p	6.2p	5.9p
Fuel (mpg)	12.8	12.9	19.2	17.8

Fig 1   Unimog winching vehicle

Fig 2   Bedford 350, four by four van

Fig 3   110 Land Rover fitted with nine metre hydraulic work platform

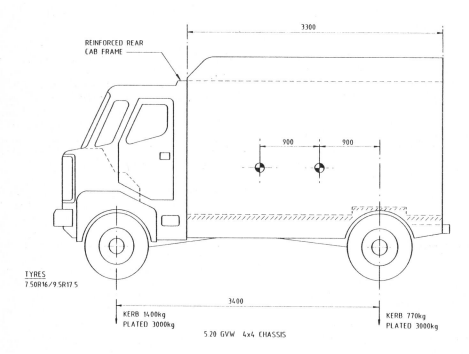

Fig 4   Outline drawing of suggested 5.2 tonne GWV chassis

Further developments in four-wheel drive transmissions

P W R STUBBS, BSc(Tech) and D GOODWIN, BSc(Eng) PhD
Land Rover Limited, Solihull, West Midlands

SYNOPSIS Further developments of four-wheel drive transmissions for on/off road vehicles are described. These include a new heavy duty five-speed manual gearbox and an adaption of a four-speed automatic gearbox, in addition to enhancements to existing transmissions.

1 INTRODUCTION

At Drive Line 84, the authors described a new range of transmissions designed and developed specifically for four-wheel drive on/off road vehicles (1).

At that time, the first phase of the range of new products had been introduced to the market in the form of the One-Ten and Ninety Land Rovers and the substantially updated Range Rover offering five-speed manual gearbox or three-speed automatic transmission.

This paper describes further major transmission developments introduced since then and the functional requirements and design philosophies upon which they were based.

2 TRANSMISSION REQUIREMENTS

The first phase of new transmission design and development had resulted in:

- a five-speed synchromesh main gearbox, the LT77, for use in all 4-cylinder Land Rovers and also the V8 Range Rover.

- an adaption of the Chrysler 727 TorqueFlite automatic transmission as an alternative to LT77 in Range Rover.

- a new versatile two-speed transfer gearbox, the LT230, offering a range of ratios, suitable for all the above applications and including a lockable inter-axle differential.

Two further requirements were identified:

- a five-speed manual main gearbox and accompanying transfer box suitable for the very heaviest duty Land Rover applications behind the V8 engine.

- an extended ratio range for the automatic transmission in Range Rover to improve still further both on-road economy and off-road manoeuvreability.

How these requirements were met, together with further enhancements of the existing transmissions, are described in greater detail in the following chapters.

3 HEAVY DUTY 5-SPEED GEARBOX (LT85)

The requirement to extend the use of five-speed overdrive manual gearboxes into the V8 Land Rover had long been foreseen. Extensive design studies, confirmed by rig testing, showed that the durability of the LT77 gearbox would be unacceptably compromised if it were to be used for the heaviest duties behind the V8 engine in Land Rover and that, therefore, a larger unit would be needed for this application.

The existing LT95 4-speed transmission first described in ref.2 had given good service over many years in V8 Land Rovers, but was not readily convertible to five-speeds; moreover it had an integral transfer box which no longer matched the production facilities developed around the universal application of the separate LT230 unit.

A design existed for a new five-speed main gearbox based on the LT95 unit and prototypes had been run successfully, but it had never been put into production. Designated the LT85, it offered a potential answer to the need for a heavier duty five-speed unit.

Figure 1 shows the general arrangement of the transmission. The ratio range is:

First	3.65 :1
Second	2.18 :1
Third	1.44 :1
Fourth	1.00 :1
Fifth	0.79 :1

The unit is a conventional three shaft design with Warner type synchromesh on all forward gears. The bearing arrangements are a conventional combination of ball and roller elements with the fifth gear pair mounted behind the rear bearing set. Selection is from a lever mounted on the top cover acting on a four rail system giving a four plane gate with reverse alongside first and fifth alongside third.

An important feature of the gearbox for very heavy duty applications is the provision of pumped oil feed to the bearings under the mainshaft gears and in the spigot between input and output shafts. The pump is housed in the front cover and picks up oil through a serviceable filter mounted integrally with the drain plug.

The fifth gear pair is housed in an adaptor casing which connects the main casing to that of the LT230 transfer box. All the mainshaft gears are mounted via needle roller bearings on the mainshaft which has a splined extension which mates with the transfer box input gear on assembly.

The gearbox is suitable for inputs up to 300 Nm (220 lb ft) in 4x4 vehicles up to 4 tonne GVW.

4   DEVELOPMENT OF LT77 5-SPEED GEARBOX

The LT77 gearbox, as described in Ref.1, had given good service during the first two years of its use in 4x4 vehicles in both Land Rover and Range Rover. The design of the remote control used in both applications had been constrained mainly by the requirements of the Land Rover application and it had been recognised that given the opportunity, a different gearchange acting directly could offer improved shift ergonomics on Range Rover.

The opportunity to do this came with the substantial interior changes planned for the 1986 model year. The general arrangement of the gearbox is shown in Figure 2 which shows the new direct acting gear lever mounted in the adaptor casing between it and the transfer box.

In addition, another version of the gearbox, this time without a transfer box, had been developed for light commercial vehicles. This features a direct acting gearchange and an extra wide ratio range required for light commercial vehicle operation. It includes similar technical features to the 4x4 versions of the gearbox, including the oil pump and filter. In this application, the filter is a large capacity nylon mesh unit designed to need no service during the life of the vehicle.

The LT77 also continues to be used in a number of passenger car applications including the Rover SD1 luxury saloon for which it was originally designed, in taxis, and in a number of specialist high performance sports cars. The range of ratios available in the various applications of the LT77 gearbox is as follows:

	Range Rover	Land Rover	Freight Rover	Cars
First	3.32:1	3.59:1	3.99:1	3.32:1
Second	2.13:1	2.30:1	2.52:1	2.09:1
Third	1.40:1	1.51:1	1.51:1	1.40:1
Fourth	1.00:1	1.00:1	1.00:1	1.00:1
Fifth	0.77:1	0.83:1	0.83:1	0.79:1
Reverse	3.54:1	3.70:1	3.70:1	3.54:1

5   ZF 4HP22 AUTOMATIC GEARBOX

The Chrysler 727 gearbox had proved very robust in Range Rover and had demonstrated the advantages of an automatic transmission in terms of ease of control, in both on and off road conditions.

It was known that a transmission with a wider ratio range and a torque converter lock-up clutch would further enhance both off-road performance and on-road economy.

Transmissions to this specification were available, but packaging constraints prevented their use until the arrival of the ZF 4HP22, first used in BMW 700 series cars in 1983. This transmission is described fully in Ref.3. It consists of a 3 element torque converter of conventional geometry but containing within its casing a self-contained, hydraulically-actuated lock-up clutch and torsionally flexible coupling. The torque converter specification depends on the application, and in Range Rover it is a 280mm diameter unit having a stall torque ratio of 2.25:1. The Simpson type epicyclic gearset provides four forward ratios and reverse as follows:

First	2.48 :1
Second	1.48 :1
Third	1.00 :1
Fourth	0.73 :1
Reverse	2.09 :1

Figure 3 shows a cross-section through the transmission.

The Range Rover provided a significantly more arduous environment for the transmission by virtue of being considerably heavier than a passenger car and having all wheels driven.

Several modifications were needed to the transmission for the Range Rover. These were designed and developed jointly by Land Rover and ZF. A special torque converter housing was needed to adapt to the Land Rover V8 engine, together with a rear adaptor casing to mate with the LT230 transfer box. These were dimensioned so that the position of the transfer box in the chassis is the same as with the manual transmission, thus permitting the use of common propellor shafts and simplifying the controls. To avoid the need for a special output shaft, the drive from the ZF unit into the transfer box is taken by loose extension shaft splined to the standard ZF mainshaft at the front and the transfer box at the rear. A deeper sump with lowered oil pick-up was needed to permit operation on extreme gradients and a strengthened parking pawl was developed to restrain the vehicle under all conditions.

An oil/air heat exchanger is installed in front of the main engine radiator to restrict maximum transmission oil temperature under arduous conditions, whilst an oil temperature warning light provides visual indication of potential damage under abuse conditions such as for instance if the driver has failed to select low transfer ratio when necessary.

The tune of the transmission was developed to provide optimum shift quality and shift points, and an uprated forward main clutch pack was developed to provide adequate durability under the most arduous conditions.

The wider ratio spread of the transmission has permitted the use of a lower high range in the transfer box, whilst at the same time raising the gearing in top gear from 37.8 km/h (23.6 mph) per 1000 rpm engine speed (nominal) to 43.2 (27.0) with locked up converter, with corresponding improvements in cruising fuel consumption. At the other end of the scale, the lower transfer box ratio has provided enhanced acceleration and gradient performance in high range.

6 UPRATED LR230 TRANSFER BOX

The availability of the LT85 main gearbox as described in Chapter 3, mandated a corresponding uprating of the LT230 transfer box. Tests confirmed that the gears possessed adequate margins of strength, but showed that attention would be needed to the bearing arrangements for the intermediate gear cluster and the high/low engagement dogs.

The dog teeth were strengthened simply by making them longer. This was achieved by moving the output gears apart and at the same time, the neutral position was widened to make it more positive to assist shifting in the transfer box.

The needle roller bearing and thrust washers carrying the intermediate cluster were replaced by twin taper roller bearings, and the detail arrangement is shown in figure 4. The required preload is obtained by a collapsible spacer placed between the bearing cups, which is collapsed by the nut. A special machine was developed by Gardner Denver for this purpose. The machine accepts the partly assembled transfer box which at this stage has the input gear installed and the intermediate cluster loosely assembled. The machine rotates the intermediate cluster at 1 RPM via the input gear and continuously monitors the torque required so to do. The same machine then tightens the nut until the input torque rises by a predetermined amount indicating that the required torque-to-turn and hence bearing preload has been achieved. The nut is then staked. The machine monitors input torque and rejects the unit if either the initial input torque is out of limits, or if the specified final torque-to-turn is not achieved within a given range of nut tightening torques. This procedure effectively addresses the important preload requirement of taper roller bearings.

7 CONCLUSION

This paper has described the extensive transmission engineering programme undertaken to enhance and expand the range of gearboxes and transfer boxes specified by Land Rover Limited. The programme reflects the continuing demand for on-road performance, economy and refinement whilst maintaining the durability and flexibility required for cross-country use.

ACKNOWLEDGEMENTS

The authors would like to thank the Directors of Land Rover Limited for permission to publish this paper; and personnel of Transmission Department who were involved in the projects described. The authors also acknowledge the permission of ZF to reproduce Figure 3.

REFERENCES

1   GOODWIN, C. and STUBBS, P W R. Recent Developments in Four-Wheel Drive Transmissions. Conf. Instn. Mech. Engrs. Driveline 1984. C7/84. I Mech E London 1984.

2   ADSHEAD, H. Manual Gearboxes - Cross Country Vehicles, Proc. Instn. Mech. Engrs, 1969-70, Vol 184, Pt 31.

3   DACH, H. Entwicklung des Viergang-Automatikgetriebes 4 HP 22 der ZF. ATZ June 1983.

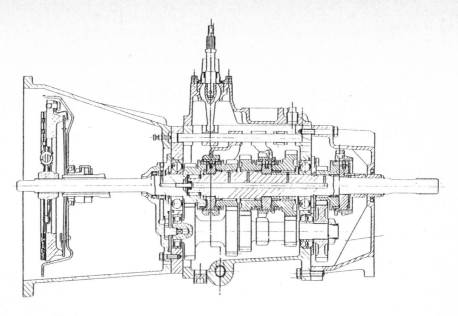

Fig 1   General arrangement of LT85 five-speed gearbox

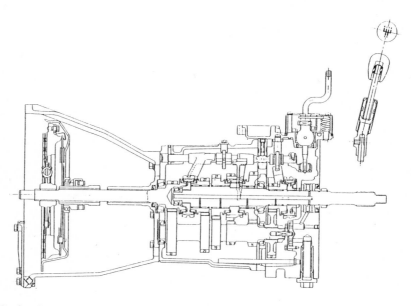

Fig 2   General arrangement of LT77 five-speed gearbox with direct gear change

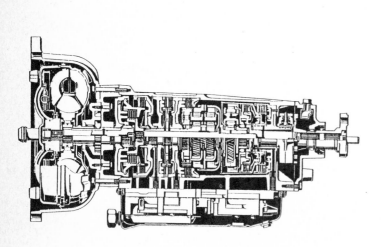

Fig 3   General arrangement of ZF 4HP22 automatic transmission

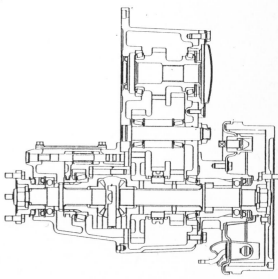

Fig 4   General arrangement of uprated LT230 transfer box

A computer controlled transfer in Toyota Hi-Lux four-wheel drive model

K FUKUMURA, BE, **Y TAGA**, ME, **S NISHIKAWA** and **K YOSHIZAWA**, BE
Toyota Motor Corporation, Aichi, Japan

SYNOPSIS
This paper discusses the analysis of transfer shift quality and some methods to control transfer shift. The new transfer developed for the TOYOTA Hi-Lux 4WD model is coupled with a computer controlled four-speed automatic transmission. This transfer makes transfer gear ratio changes possible during vehicle cruising by employing two wet-clutches and a wet-brake with a clutch-to-clutch shift mechanism replacing the conventional dog-clutches. In order to obtain smooth transfer shift quality, computer simulations for the effects of the changes of driving condition on the shift characteristics were conducted. And timing valves and double chamber constructions were introduced to this transfer based on the analysis. Additionally the computer controlled system was developed to obtain smooth transfer shift quality. These new shift control methods have been successfully applied in TOYOTA's Computer Controlled Transfer.

1   INTRODUCTION

In recent years, four-wheel driven vehicles with automatic transmissions have been well-received because of their easy driveability handling.
But in regard to the transfer shift, there still remains an operational difficulty due to the difficulty of the gear ratio changes of the transfer during vehicle cruising. In order to change the gear ratio of conventional transfer, it is necessary for the drivers to stop their vehicles and change the transmission shift lever to 'N' or 'P' position. This is caused by the application of dog-clutches. The newly developed transfer solved this problem by employing two wet-clutches with a clutch-to-clutch shift mechanism replacing the conventional dog-clutches (1)*.

The transfer shift is made available by changing the transfer shift lever position even while the vehicle is cruising, and can occur over a wide range of transfer input torques, input revolution rates and vehicle speeds. In order to obtain smooth shift quality, it is important to understand quantitatively the shift characteristics under all the various driving conditions.

This paper discusses the analysis of transfer shift quality and some methods to control transfer shift.

* Numbers in parentheses designate References at end of this paper.

2 CONSTRUCTION

Fig.1 shows a cross-sectional view of the new transfer mechanism along with the transmission. The transfer is located at the rear of the transmission, and contains a High-Low shift and a 2WD-4WD shift.

Principal sections of this transfer are as follows;

1. A single planetary gear set for reduction
2. Two wet-clutches and a wet-brake for High-Low shift and 2WD-4WD shift
3. A chain which transfers the drive forward to the front wheels
4. An electro-hydraulic control unit
5. Transfer shift lever whose positions are composed of 'H2', 'H4' and 'L4'

Fig.2 shows the schematic layout of the transfer. Table 1 illustrates the clutch operations in various conditions. This transfer adopts a clutch-to-clutch shift mechanism. The direct drive is available when C3 clutch is engaged and B4 brake is disengaged. The power from the transmission output shaft is directly conveyed to the transfer output shaft through the sun gear, C3 clutch and planetary carrier. The reduction drive is available when C3 clutch is disengaged and B4 brake is engaged. In this case, the power is provided through the sun gear, planetary pinion and carrier. And the resultant gear ratio is 2.66. Further, C4 clutch is engaged for the four-wheel drive mode, in which the power is conveyed to the front output shaft passing through the C4 clutch, drive sprocket, chain and driven sprocket.

Both the transmission and the transfer are controlled by a single computer. We applied the electro-hydraulic system which we developed in order to control the transmission (2). In terms of the signals to and from the computer, a transfer shift position sensor and one solenoid valve are introduced to this transfer application. The transfer shift position sensor has functions including detection of the transfer low range in the 'L4' position. The solenoid valve is fixed in the electro-hydraulic unit and is actuated to change the transfer gear ratio. The computer has a particular shift pattern for transfer low range, which is designed to create the maximum drive force in each transmission gear ratio.

3 ANALYSIS OF TRANSFER SHIFT QUALITY

Fig.3 shows the characteristics of revolution
rates for transfer planetary gear members and
pressures during the transfer shift. During the
High to Low shift, just after C3 clutch is
released, the revolution of the sun gear gains
in rate while that of the ring gear loses with
the engine revving up. In order to obtain High
to Low smooth shift quality, it is required to
properly underlap the timing between C3 clutch
release and B4 brake engagement. Namely, it is
important to understand quantitatively the
interval betwwen C3 clutch release and the
moment the ring gear revolution rate decreases
to zero. We abbreviate this interval as 'Proper
interval'. In the case of Low to High shift,
the timing overlap between B4 brake release and
C3 clutch engagement is highly critical. And in
this case, the shift quality depends on the
torque capacity of C3 clutch at the moment B4
brake is released. Therefore, it is important
to understand quantitatively the necessary
pressure on C3 clutch that is required to
prevent the engine from over-revving and to
prevent output torque fluctuation when B4 brake
is released. We abbreviate this pressure on C3
clutch as 'Required pressure'.

The quantitative analysis for above 'Proper
interval' and 'Required pressure' under various
conditions of throttle opening, vehicle speed
and transmission gear ratio were conducted with
a computer. The schematic layout in Fig.4
shows a model for simulation of this transmission
and transfer. This model is divided into ten
members represented by the symbols I_1 to I_{10}.

The equations of motion on each member are
as follows;

$$T_E - T_p - T_{L/C} - I_1 \dot{\omega}_E = 0 \tag{1}$$

$$T_{L/C} + T_t - T_{FO} - T_{CO} + T_{OP,Ca} - I_2 \dot{\omega}_t = 0 \tag{2}$$

$$T_{CO} - T_{BO} + T_{FO} - T_{OP,S} - I_3 \dot{\omega}_{OP,S} = 0 \tag{3}$$

$$-T_{OP,R} - T_{C_2} - T_{FP,R} - I_4 \dot{\omega}_{FP,R} = 0 \tag{4}$$

$$T_{C_2} + T_{B_1} + T_{F_1} - T_{FP,S} - T_{RP,S} - I_5 \dot{\omega}_{FP,S} = 0 \tag{5}$$

$$T_{B_2} - T_{F_1} - I_6 \dot{\omega}_{F_1} = 0 \tag{6}$$

$$T_{FP,Ca} - T_{RP,R} - T_{C_3} - T_{TP,S} - I_7 \dot{\omega}_{TP,S} = 0 \tag{7}$$

$$T_{F_2} + T_{B_3} + T_{RP,Ca} - I_8 \dot{\omega}_{RP,Ca} = 0 \tag{8}$$

$$T_{B_4} - T_{TP,R} - I_9 \dot{\omega}_{TP,R} = 0 \tag{9}$$

$$T_{C_3} + T_{TP,Ca} - T_o - I_{10} \dot{\omega}_o = 0 \tag{10}$$

The general equations for torques and
revolutions of planetaty gear members are as
follows;

$$T_{Ca} = (1-b) T_R = \frac{b-1}{b} T_S \tag{11}$$

$$b\omega_S - \omega_R + (1-b)\omega_{Ca} = 0 \tag{12}$$

$$b = -\frac{Z_S}{Z_R} \tag{13}$$

where; subscripts
 T = torque
 I = inertia
 ω = angular velocity

Z = number of teeth
E = engine
p = pump member of torque converter
t = turbine member of torque converter
L/C = lock-up-clutch
F = overrunning clutch
OP = overdrive planetary gear
FP = front planetary gear
RP = rear planetary gear
TP = transfer planetary gear
R = ring gear
S = sun gear
Ca = carrier member
CO = overdrive direct clutch
C1 = forward clutch
C2 = direct clutch
C3 = transfer direct clutch
C4 = transfer front drive clutch
BO = overdrive brake
B1 = second coast brake
B2 = second brake
B3 = first and reverse brake
B4 = transfer low speed brake
o = output member

The foregoing equations of motion are
solved by a computer. The input data are the
hydraulic pressures applied to the C3 clutch
and B4 brake with respect to time. The shift
characteristics such as changes of transfer
output torque, engine speed, torque and speed
of every rotating member of the transmission and
the transfer can be computed (3).

Fig.5 shows the experimental results,
where the broken lines represent the computed
shift characteristics of the vehicle. It can
be seen from the figure that the computed
results show good agreement with the
experiments.

The characteristics of the foregoing 'Proper
interval' and 'Required pressure' under various
conditions of throttle opening, vehicle speed and
transmission gear ratio are shown in Figs.6(a) and
(b) respectively. As is obvious from these
figures, both 'Proper interval' and 'Required
pressure' are over a wide range, and the bigger
the gear ratio of the transmission the wider are
these ranges. Figs.7(a) and (b) show the results
of the computation for the effect of the timing
between two clutch engagements on the shift
characteristics. In the case of High to Low
shift as shown in Fig.7(a), if B4 brake is
engaged too fast (that is, too much overlap),
the output torque will change to a negative
state. And if it is engaged too slowly (that is,
too much underlap), the engine will rev up and
the output torque will subsequently show a
fluctuation. In case of Low to High shift as
shown in Fig.7(b), if B4 brake is released too
fast before C3 clutch is applied (that is, too
much underlap), the engine will rev up. And if
it is released after C3 is applied (that is, too
much overlap), the output torque will drop
severely.

It was proved that a slight error of the
timing between two clutch engagements caused
undesirable shift characteristics, and the
development of new shift control methods were
essential to obtain smooth shift quality and
satisfactory completion of this transfer.

4 TRANSFER SHIFT CONTROL METHODS

The following three control methods were introduced to this transfer in addition to the conventional methods (such as accumulator, cushion plate etc.).

4.1 Timing valves

(1) H-L ORIFICE CONTROL VALVE

As the throttle opening increases, a faster engaging of B4 brake is required (Fig.6(a)). The H-L ORIFICE CONTROL VALVE (Fig.8(a)) works to change the oil volume flowing into B4 brake by three different steps according to the throttle openings. When the throttle opening is narrow (see Table 2) the oil flows through OR1 and OR2 in series. When it is medium, the oil flows through the series of OR1 and OR2 and the series of OR1 and OR3 in parallel. And when it is wide, the oil flows only through OR1. The characteristics of pressure are shown in Fig.8(b).

(2) L-H SHIFT TIMING VALVE

This valve was introduced in order to properly overlap the timing between B4 brake release and C3 clutch engagement. As is shown in Fig.9(a), the pressure on C3 clutch is applied at the top of this valve through port A. When the pressure on C3 clutch reaches a predetermined level, this valve moves to the lower position to release B4 brake immediately by exhausting the pressure through port B and C. The characteristics of pressure are shown in Fig.9(b).

4.2 Double chamber construction

The torque that should be transmitted by C3 clutch or B4 brake varies in a wide range. To cope with this situation, a double chamber construction (Fig.10(a)) was introduced to both C3 clutch and B4 brake. With this construction, the first chamber is filled with oil faster than the second one. And the consolidated torque capacity of the clutch will increase with filling of the second chamber. This enables the clutch to cover the transmission of torque in a wide range. The characteristics of pressures being applied to both chambers and consolidated torque capacity are shown in Fig.10(b).

4.3 Computer control

The computer shift range for High to Low shift is shown in Fig.11(a). In this figure, High to Low shift is available in A and B regions, but not in other regions. These ranges are preprogrammed to eliminate the engine over-rev range and to obtain smooth shift quality and durability.

One of the features of this computer controlled system is that when the transfer shift lever is manually selected to 'L4' position under the condition in which the states of throttle opening and vehicle speed are in the A region shown in Fig.11(a) with the transmission being in the first gear, the transmission moves to the second gear first keeping the transfer in High state. And after the proper interval of time the transfer moves to Low state (Fig.11(b)). Besides, after the transfer shift has been completed the transmission returns to the proper gear. It is the purpose of this control to obtain reduction of the transfer input torque momentarily and to stabilize shift characteristics by decreasing the foregoing 'Proper interval'. In the case of Low to High shift, the computer controlled system was introduced in the same way as High to Low shift.

As the transfer shift is manually selected, there is a possibility that a shift could occur simultaneously in both the transfer and the transmission. This would cause the line pressure to fall, damaging friction plates with a resultant poor shift quality. To avoid this, the control system is so designed that the computer gives proper instructions for sequential shift, precisely determining the right intervals for the transmission and the transfer.

5 RESULTS

Figs.12 and 13 show the computed results. In both figures, (b) shows the effects obtained by applying the methods as described above. In the shaded area smooth shift quality is obtained. By comparing figure (b) with (a), it can be seen that application of the foregoing methods enables the shaded area to greatly increase. And transfer shift quality is smooth enough for practical usage.

Fig.14 shows typical experimental shift characteristics obtained by applying the new control system. It is seen from these figures that smooth shift quality was obtained in both High to Low and Low to High shift. Similar results were obtained under the other conditions.

6 CONCLUSIONS

1. This new transfer construction makes transfer gear ratio changes possible during vehicle cruising.
2. It was proved that the new shift control methods required consideration of such changeable factors as throttle opening, vehicle speed and transmission gear ratio to obtain smooth shift quality.
3. Timing valves, double chamber constructions and computer controlled system were developed based on the analysis. And these new shift control methods have been successfully applied in TOYOTA's Computer Controlled Transfer.

REFERENCES

1. S. Moroto, K. Kobayashi, Y. Hayakawa, S. Kubo; "A Computer Controlled Transfer for Four-Wheel Drive Vehicles", paper 850354 presented at SAE International Congress & Exposition, Detroit, February 25-March 1, 1985.

2. Y. Taga, K. Nakamura, H. Ito, T. Taniguchi; "TOYOTA Computer Controlled Four-Speed Automatic Transmission", paper 820740 presented at SAE Passenger Car Meeting, Troy, June 7-10, 1982.

3. Y. Shindo, H. Ito, T. Ishihara; "A Fundamental Consideration on Shift Mechanism of Automatic Transmission", paper 790043 presented at SAE Congress and Exposition, Detroit, February 26-March 2, 1979.

Table 1   Clutch operations

Position	Drive mode	C_3	B_4	C_4	Gear ratio
H2	2WD direct drive	O			1.00
H4	4WD direct drive	O		O	1.00
L4	4WD reduction drive		O	O	2.66

Table 2   Flow path

Stage	Throttle opening	Flow path
1	Narrow	→ OR1 → OR2 →
2	Medium	OR1 → OR2 / OR1 → OR3
3	Wide	→ OR1 →

Automatic transmission   **Transfer**

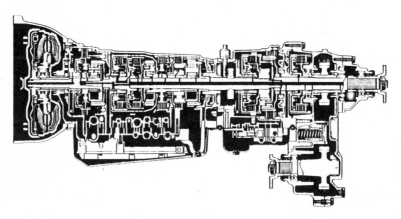

Fig 1   Sectional view of the transmission and the transfer

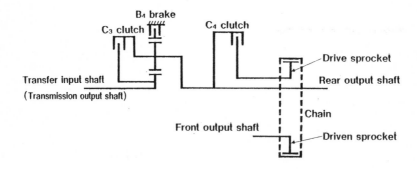

Fig 2   Schematic layout of the transfer

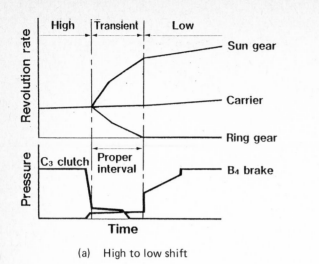

(a)   High to low shift

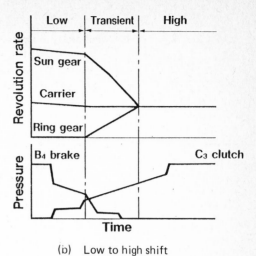

(b)   Low to high shift

Fig 3   Characteristics of revolution rate and pressure
during transfer shift

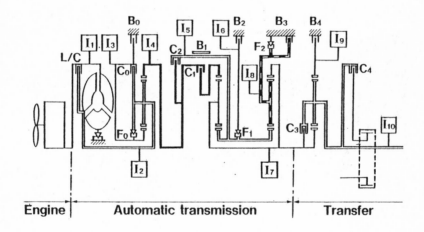

Fig 4   Schematic layout (simulation model)

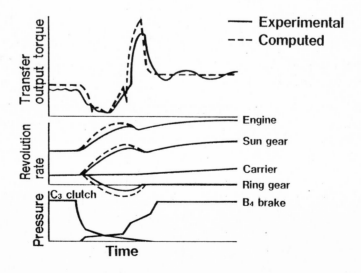

Fig 5   Shift characteristics during high to low shift

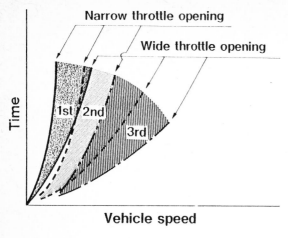

(a) High to low shift

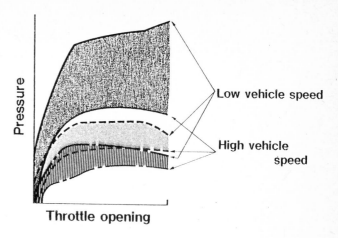

(b) Low to high shift

Fig 6   Characteristics of 'proper interval' and 'required pressure'

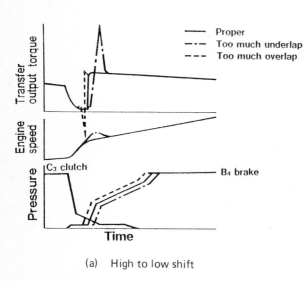

(a) High to low shift

(b) Low to high shift

Fig 7   Effects of the timing between two clutch engagements on the shift characteristics

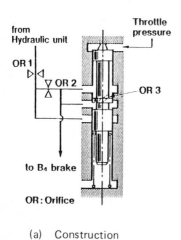

(a) Construction

(b) Characteristics of pressure

Fig 8   H—L orifice control valve

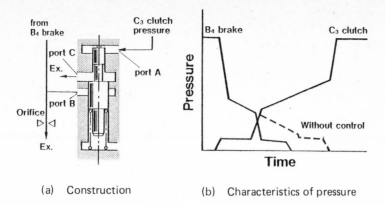

(a) Construction   (b) Characteristics of pressure

Fig 9   L—H shift timing valve

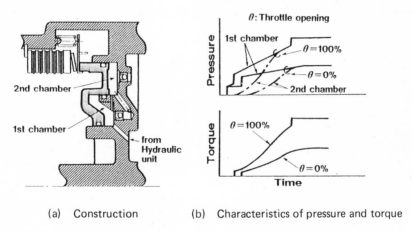

(a)   Construction   (b)   Characteristics of pressure and torque

Fig 10 Double chamber construction

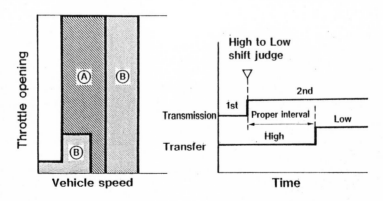

(a)   Shift range for high to low shift   (b)   Sequential control

Fig 11 Computer control

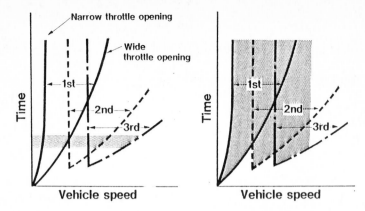

(a) Before applying counter-measures (b) After applying counter-measures

Fig 12 Computed results for high to low shift

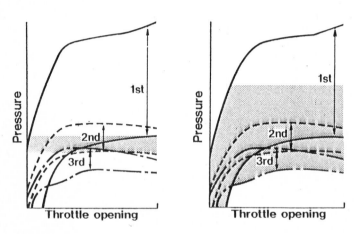

(a) Before applying counter-measures (b) After applying counter-measures

Fig 13 Computed results for low to high shift

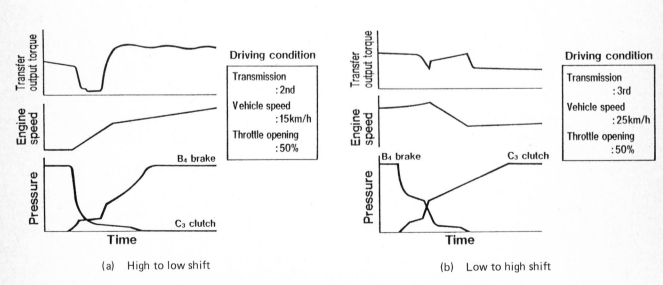

(a) High to low shift

(b) Low to high shift

Fig 14 Typical experimental shift characteristics

C12/86

Integral ball bearing spindles for front-wheel drive and four-wheel drive vehicles

D G TEREK, BSME and **P J CHRISTIANSEN**, BME
General Motors Corporation, Sandusky, Ohio, USA

<u>Synopsis</u>   This paper discusses various types of automotive wheel bearings, construction details and advantages of front and rear wheel New Departure Hyatt integral ball bearing spindles, current production applications of New Departure Hyatt integral ball bearing spindles, and modifications that were made to an automotive front wheel spindle for use on a light duty four wheel drive utility truck.

Types of Automotive Wheel Bearings

The primary purpose of this paper is to discuss fully integral ball bearing spindles that are used in many front and rear wheel automotive applications in the United States. Typical spindles are shown in Figures 1 and 2 and as discussed later, have ball races integral with two flanged components, the stationary hub, or outer ring, and the rotating spindle, or inner ring.

For definition however, and for enhancement of the reader's understanding of wheel bearings in general, the authors include herein a brief discussion of some of the other types of automotive wheel bearings that are used throughout the world today. Included are semi-integral designs, cartridge double row designs and single row designs.

Semi-integral bearings, Figures 3, 4, and 5, have two ball races or pathways integral with one flanged component, the outer ring, and conventional inner rings that are mounted on a rotating drive axle, Figure 3 and 5, or on a stationary spindle, Figure 4. Semi-integral ball, Figures 3 and 4, and tapered roller, Figure 5, designs exist. Bearing manufacturers supply a flanged outer ring/inner ring subassembly that is assembled by the user to a flanged shaft that mates with the inner ring(s).

Cartridge double row bearings, Figures 6 and 7, have two rows of rolling elements and straight diameter inner and outer rings with no flanges. They are assembled by the user into a knuckle bore and onto a rotating drive axle. Cartridge double row ball and tapered roller bearing designs exist.

Many rear wheel drive vehicles today use the "direct-on" single row cylindrical roller bearing configuration that was introduced in the 1960's, Figure 8. This overall design was the beginning of the evolution to integrate bearing components into the system by eliminating conventional inner rings. Note that the cylindrical rollers ride on a bearing pathway that has been ground directly on a surface of the drive axle.

Single row bearings are used on many driven wheel, Figure 9, and drive wheel, Figure 10, positions today. Bearing manufacturers supply two single row bearings and the user procures and assembles all of the other components, including greasing and adjusting endplay.

A review of these types of wheel bearings indicates that as one moves toward the fully integral designs shown in Figures 1 and 2 from the single row, the cartridge double row or the semi-integral designs, fewer mating parts are required for a completed assembly. This results in decreasing the number of surfaces to be fabricated, decreasing the cost of assembly, and increasing the overall reliability of the final assembly.

Construction and Material Details of NDH Integral Ball Bearing Spindles

Front and rear wheel integral ball bearing spindles (Figures 1 and 2) are precision bearings consisting of:

1. A structural stationary hub which is bolted to the vehicle's suspension system
2. A rotating spindle on which are mounted vehicle brake and wheel components
3. Two rows of angular contact ball bearings
4. Seals
5. Grease
6. Splines (on the drive wheel designs)
7. Keeper rings, retainers, and dust caps (on the driven wheel designs)

Both outer ball races are integral with the hub and one inner ball race is integral with the spindle. This integration of ball races with structural components of a vehicle's suspension system increases overall system reliability by reducing the number of critical surfaces required to interface between the bearing and the rest of the assembly. Note that there are no conventional outer and inner rings in these components, thereby eliminating the need to fabricate and to control critical dimensions, in knuckles, in brake rotors and on drive axles.

Integrating ball races with the hub and spindle also reduces assembly weight and increases system strength for a given space restriction or annulus in which to fit a bearing for a given application. System performance is improved by increasing the accuracy of the rotating flange on the spindle on which brake and wheel components are mounted. Brake pulsations and wheel wobble and eccentricity are improved by the concentricity and axial runout of the brake and wheel mounting surfaces to the axis of rotation.

The material selected for the hubs and spindles is SAE-AISI 1070 modified, electric furnace quality, carbon vacuum deoxidized, bearing quality steel produced to stringent internal cleanliness requirements. Significant improvements in fatigue life have been achieved with the cooperation of steel producers in an NDH initiated program to reduce the size and frequency of non-metallic micro and macro-inclusions. The steel industry has adopted an NDH developed rating system that reflects micro-inclusion frequency as well as severity. Hubs and spindles are machined from forgings that are made from heats of steel approved by NDH prior to use. Surfaces subjected to rolling contact and/or bending fatigue are selectively induction hardened to maximize fatigue life while providing ductile mounting surfaces and a shock resistant core.

A separable inner ring is press fitted on the spindle and its ball race is finished at the same time as the integral spindle ball race for maximum accuracy. It is made from through hardened 52100 steel produced to the same internal cleanliness requirements mentioned above for the 1070 hub and spindle material.

On the driven wheel design the inner ring is retained axially by the press fit and by keeper rings and a retainer. On the drive wheel design the inner ring is retained by the press fit and by an axial clamp load applied through the inner ring/spindle shoulder by the drive axle assembly.

Through-hardened 52100 balls are selected after gaging the outer and inner ball races to obtain the desired internal fitup. Ball sizes selected for driven wheel spindles result in preloaded assemblies with no endplay. Drive wheel spindles are assembled with endplay which decreases when clamped axially by the drive axle.

Balls are loaded into non-metallic ball separators immediately after size selection on an assembly machine station that places the ball/separator subassemblies with the specific hub and spindle for which they were selected. The separators are made from glass filled nylon for dimensional stability and to withstand elevated temperatures.

Each driven wheel assembly contains one seal on the inboard side. Each drive wheel spindle contains two seals, one on the inboard and one on the outboard side. The seal material is temperature resistant to withstand the heat input from brake components mounted on the rotating spindle. The seal material is ethylene acrylic which is used instead of nitriles because of the elevated temperatures and which

is used instead of other high temperature compounds like polyacrylates, silicones, epichlorohydrins and fluoroelastomers because it has improved low temperature flexibility, tear strength, abrasion resistance, water resistance, and/or corrosion properties.

The grease was selected to be compatible with the seal compound, to withstand elevated temperatures, to provide protection against shipping damage and corrosion, and to support the loads encountered in wheel bearing applications. Lithium and polyurea base greases are used in NDH integral ball bearing spindles. New greases are approved for production use only after extensive laboratory and vehicle four season test programs to assure long term performance.

Each spindle is assembled with bolts to attach the brake and wheel components to the rotating spindle.

The outside diameter of the dust cap on the driven wheel designs is coated with a sealant to prevent leakage of grease and ingress of contaminants into the assembly.

The overall design and construction of drive and driven integral ball bearing spindles manufactured by New Departure Hyatt eliminate the need for periodic field service. The bearings are factory adjusted and lubricated for life and do not require customer maintenance.

Production Applications

NDH integral ball bearing spindles were used for the first time on the front and rear wheel positions of General Motors 1979 E-cars and have been used on all new GM front wheel drive vehicle programs since then.

Table 1 lists 1979 through 1985 production applications for NDH integral ball bearing spindles, showing the car body code designation, the commercial name plate designation, the front and rear axle rating and the dynamic radial and thrust load rating of the wheel bearings used on these vehicles. The bearing load capacity ratings are for radial loads centered between the ball rows and for thrust loads applied on the bearing centerline. (In reality of course the loads are not applied exactly between the ball rows or on the centerline, being influenced by wheel offset, tire rolling radius, vehicle center of gravity, etc.) The bearing load capacity ratings are based on a 500 r/min, 3000 hour, B-10 life.

Tables 2 and 3 show external dimensions of the front and rear wheel bearings, respectively, that are used on these production applications.

Laboratory Fatigue Testing and Actual Vehicle Performance Data

All NDH integral ball bearing spindles are subjected to a variety of laboratory test programs prior to use on production vehicles. One of these is a durability test aimed at determining the rolling contact fatigue life of the bearing using the vehicle parameters of axle rating, wheel offset, tire rolling radius, center of gravity etc. While rotating at the equivalent of 100 miles per hour, the bearing is subjected to a constant radial load of 125% of the load it would see from the axle rating. Thrust loading is cycled over a five minute period with no load for one minute, 0.3g inward thrust load for 1.5 minutes, no load for one minute and 0.2g outward thrust load for 1.5 minutes. A lot of forty bearings is commonly run in ten sudden death groups of four bearings to establish the B10 fatigue life for the application. A minimum B10 life of 200 hours is required and was obtained for each of the applications shown in Table 1.

Perhaps of more interest to the reader is actual vehicle performance data. A recent study of twelve month replacement rates for some of the applications shown in Table 1 is summarized below:

	Front Wheel	Rear Wheel
E-K Cars	0.29%	0.16%
X Car	0.49%	0.09%
A Car	0.49%	0.07%
J Car	0.42%	0.06%
T Truck	0.39%	N.A.

Note that front wheel bearing replacement is slightly higher than rear wheel bearing replacement on these vehicles. Front wheel bearings are influenced by two parameters that do not affect rear wheel bearings on these vehicles. A clamp load must be applied to the bearing by the drive axle and an auxiliary seal is used in the front knuckle. Insufficient clamp loading and water entry have been observed on a few of the front wheel returns.

NDH examines bearings that are replaced on customers vehicles and finds that 25-35% are OK and should not have been replaced. Insufficient clamp load, shipping damage, fatigue spalling, water entry and manufacturing errors have been observed in the few bearings that have been returned after replacement before 24000 miles.

Modifications to Automotive Bearings for Light Duty Truck Use

In 1983 General Motors introduced a light utility four wheel drive truck that required an integral ball bearing spindle for the front wheel position. Vehicle mass and front suspension design called for the use on this truck of the same front wheel bearing that was being used on the front wheel of the E-car.

Several different laboratory tests are used to validate NDH spindles for production applications, including a rotary fatigue test to evaluate the strength of the flange of the rotating spindle on which are mounted the wheel and brake components. This laboratory test is run at 300 r/min with the equivalent of 0.7 g inward thrust loading that is developed through consideration of vehicle front mass, center of gravity, tire track, tire rolling radius and wheel offset. Production wheels and brake rotors are mounted on the spindle and a test load is applied at an angle of approximately 55° to the rotating spindle. The test is run until the test machine automatically shuts down due to

deflections caused by fracture of the spindle flange.

Initial testing that was conducted approximately two years prior to vehicle introduction indicated a need to modify the E-car front wheel spindle for use under T-truck loads. Several design iterations were evaluated including changing corner form configurations, increasing flange thickness and adding an induction hardened heat treat pattern to the corner of the wheel pilot and flange face. Each of these modifications by itself yielded limited benefits, but maximum improvements were obtained by using all three design considerations. Rotary fatigue test life was improved over that obtained prior to making these design changes.

Subsequent evaluation of production components on vehicles on various Proving Ground test schedules and by finite element analysis proved that the design changes that were made and tested in the laboratory prior to production did in fact result in a reliable and durable product for this application.

Summary

New Departure Hyatt integral ball bearing spindles utilize design features that provide improved reliability, durability and performance of front and rear wheel bearings by fully integrating ball bearing rolling contact surfaces in a factory assembled, greased and sealed unit that requires no customer service. Vehicle performance is improved by the accuracy of rotating components and overall system mass and costs are minimized by design features.

Production use by General Motors has increased from one vehicle in the 1979 model year to all of GM's United States produced front wheel drive car and one four wheel drive truck programs and will continue to expand in future vehicle programs. The integrated design lends itself to design changes as needed for new vehicle programs.

Table 1 Production applications of New Departure Hyatt (NDH) integral
ball bearing spindles

BODY CODE	NAMEPLATE	VEHICLE AXLE RATING		NDH INTEGRAL BALL BEARING SPINDLE			
				RADIAL CAPACITY		THRUST CAPACITY	
		FRONT (KG)	REAR (KG)	FRONT (N)	REAR (N)	FRONT (N)	REAR (N)
E	BUICK RIVIERA OLDSMOBILE TORONADO CADILLAC ELDORADO	1152	1085	15200	14300	13500	12600
K	CADILLAC SEVILLE	1240	1140	15200	14300	13500	12600
X	BUICK SKYLARK CHEVROLET CITATION OLDSMOBILE OMEGA PONTIAC PHOENIX	946	782	11500	11200	10200	9700
A	BUICK CENTURY CHEVROLET CELEBRITY OLDSMOBILE CIERA PONTIAC 6000	981 1200	850 1030	11500 14600	13400 13400	10200 12800	11800 11800
J	BUICK SKYHAWK CADILLAC CIMARRON CHEVROLET CAVALIER OLDSMOBILE FIRENZA PONTIAC SUNBIRD	909	738	11500	11200	10200	9700
T TRK	CHEVROLET BLAZER AND S-10 PICKUP GMC JIMMY S-15 PICKUP	1247	–	15200	–	13500	–
P	PONTIAC FIERO	–	803	–	11500	–	10200
Y	CHEVROLET CORVETTE	782	880	14300	15200	12600	13500
N	BUICK SOMERSET OLDSMOBILE CALAIS PONTIAC GRAND AM	1025	760	13400	11200	10400	9700
C	BUICK ELECTRA CADILLAC DEVILLE CADILLAC FLEETWOOD OLDSMOBILE 98	1200	1020	14600	13400	12800	11800

Table 2 External dimensions — New Departure Hyatt drive wheel bearings

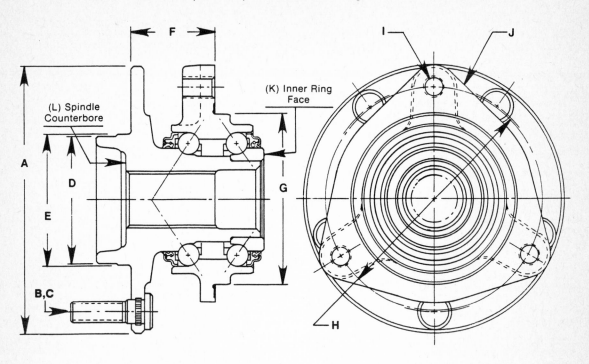

BODY	SPINDLE						HUB			
	A	B	C	D	E	F	G	H	I	J
CODE	Flange Dia.	Bolt Circle Dia.	Bolt Size (Qty.)	Wheel Pilot Dia.	Brake Pilot Dia.	Flange Offset	Hub Pilot Dia.	Bolt Circle Dia.	Bolt Hole Size (Qty.)	Flange Shape
millimeters										
X, A, P	125.00	100.00	M12x1.5 (5)	56.96	57.74	42.06	70.99	102.00	12.71 (3)	Modified Triangular
E, K, Y, T-TRK	144.50	120.65	M12x1.5 (5)	70.10	70.60	47.00	91.90	102.65	M12x1.75 (3)	Modified Triangular
A, C	147.00	115.00	M12x1.5 (5)	70.10	70.60	42.06	90.01	116.00	12.71 (3)	Modified Triangular
N	125.00	100.00	M12x1.5 (5)	56.97	58.30	44.22	73.49	98.00	12.71 (3)	Modified Triangular

SPLINE DATA
7466905, 7466925 - 33 tooth internal involute spline; 32/64 pitch, 30° P.A., 26.19375mm (1.03125") P.D.
7466920, 7466922 - 27 tooth internal involute spline; 24/48 pitch, 45° P.A., 28.575mm (1.125") P.D.

Spindles with I.D. splines require positive clamping between the inner ring face (K) and
spindle counterbore (L). Consult NDH engineering for specific torque levels.

Table 3 External dimensions — New Departure Hyatt non-drive wheel bearings

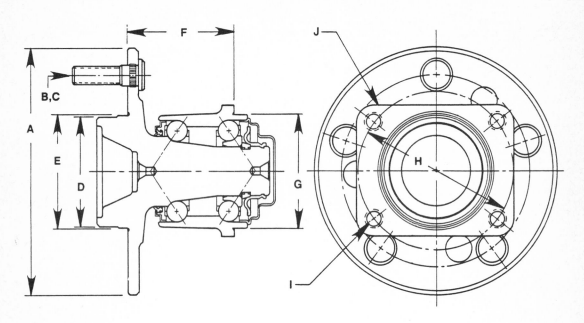

| BODY | SPINDLE | | | | | | HUB | | | |
| | A | B | C | D | E | F | G | H | I | J |
CODE	Flange Dia.	Bolt Circle Dia.	Bolt Size (Qty.)	Wheel Pilot Dia.	Brake Pilot Dia.	Flange Offset	Hub Pilot Dia.	Bolt Circle Dia.	Bolt Hole Size (Qty.)	Flange Shape
					millimeters					
E, K, Y	146.80	120.65	M12x1.5 (5)	70.10	70.60	68.72	71.76	100.60	11.57 (4)	Rectangular
X, J, N	138.00	100.00	M12x1.5 (5)	56.96	57.46	64.76	60.92	88.81	10.35 (4)	Offset Trapezoid*
A	138.00	100.00	M12x1.5 (5)	56.96	57.46	64.76	71.76	100.60	11.57 (4)	Rectangular
A, C	150.00	115.00	M12x1.5 (5)	70.10	70.60	64.76	71.76	100.60	11.70 (4)	Rectangular

*Not Shown in Illustration

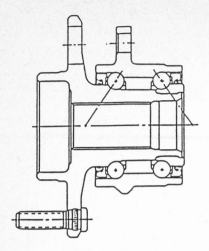

Fig 1   New Departure Hyatt ball bearing spindle — drive
         wheel

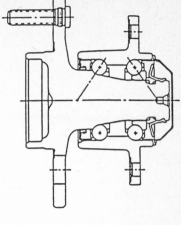

Fig 2   New Departure Hyatt ball bearing spindle — driven
         wheel

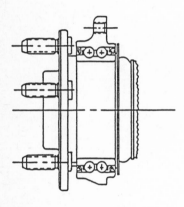

Fig 3   Semi-integral ball bearing — drive wheel

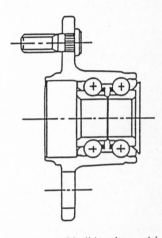

Fig 4   Semi-integral ball bearing — driven wheel

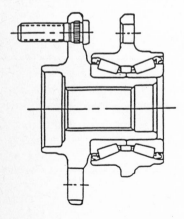

Fig 5   Semi-integral tapered roller bearing — drive wheel

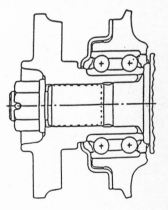

Fig 6   Cartridge double row ball bearing — drive wheel

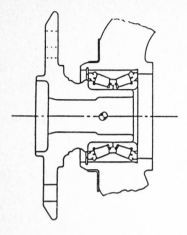

Fig 7   Cartridge double row tapered roller bearing

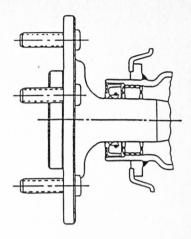

Fig 8   'Direct-on' single row cylindrical roller bearing

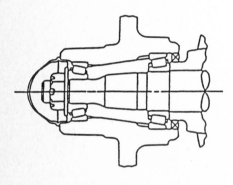

Fig 9   Single row tapered roller bearings — driven wheel

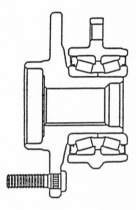

Fig 10   Single row tapered roller bearings — drive wheel